BEHAVIORAL OBJECTIVES

TEACHER SUCCESS THROUGH STUDENT PERFORMANCE

Paul D. Plowman, Ed.D.

CALIFORNIA STATE DEPARTMENT OF EDUCATION

SCIENCE RESEARCH ASSOCIATES, INC. 259 EAST ERIE STREET CHICAGO, ILLINOIS 60611
A SUBSIDIARY OF IBM

To accomplish any goal, it is desirable to have

a clear description or outline of the particular objectives

that must be met along the way.

Behavioral objectives deal with concrete, specific, measurable goals. They provide clear, precise explanations of what the learner is to do.

After reading a story concerning how a young person's values were
tested by classmates or neighbors and strengthened by the testing,
the student is to prepare a presentation with tape recorder,
colored slides, and overlays to show how reading certain books
may contribute to the development of one's values.

time of y
n yellow
ose boughs wh
re ruined choi
t birds sa

Literature and language

are woven inextricably into all learning experiences . . .

the skills of listening, speaking, reading, and writing

reinforce and enhance each other . . .

To develop understanding of importance of volunteer
services in improving the natural beauty, emergency services,
or political organizations of a community . . . each student
is to become involved in at least one volunteer service . . .

Social science presents concepts, generalizations, and

principles that help us comprehend and interpret the nature of man, the social animal.

In community studies, for example, concern should be with the dynamics

of community development, management, perpetuation, and change . . .

Students study the relationship of plant and animal life in a
balanced aquarium and determine the effect on the ecology of the
aquarium, first when 50 percent of the plant life is removed,
and second, when 50 percent of the animal life is removed . . .

Science can be viewed as a method

of organizing knowledge and of finding out about man

and everything his mind and eye perceives . . .

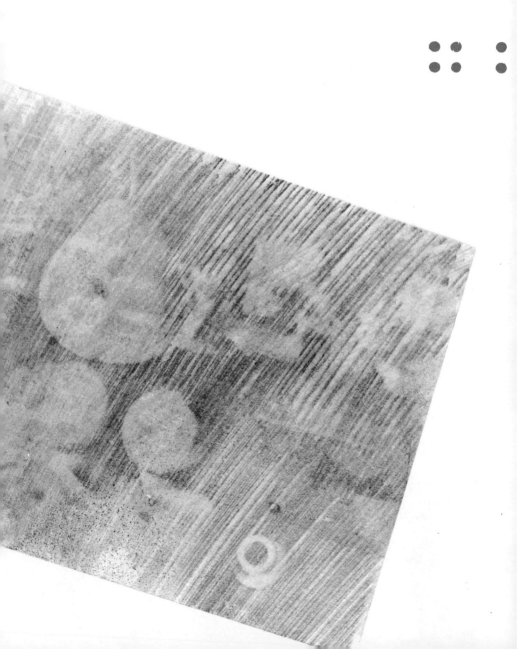

Without using a standard measuring instrument, the third grade
student is to measure the height of classmates, the dimensions of his desk,
and the length and width of his classroom and communicate
his findings to his classmates . . .

Through his fingers, a child learns differences

between symbols, solid things and mathematical terms . . .

After listening to a classical or modern musical
composition, pupils paint or draw pictures with color,
form, line, and arrangements of symbols or objects
to reflect the mood induced by the music . . .

Art and music are taught to develop a child's awareness

and powers of discrimination, analysis, and evaluation . . .

Given a breakfast menu that is deficient
in foods from one of the four basic food groups, the student
can correctly identify which food group is not represented
and suggest an appropriate addition to the menu . . .

The health curriculum must be based upon

the health needs of children and of society . . .

Design:
Fetzer Conover Graphics
San Francisco

Artist:
John Burrell

Preface

This book provides practical suggestions for formulating behavioral objectives in eight curricular areas. It contains numerous examples of these objectives and sequences of objectives for primary, middle grade, junior high school, and high school students. The methodology proposed is equally applicable to colleges, universities, and other institutions of learning.

Through adroit use of behavioral objectives, it is possible to make fundamental improvement in both teaching and learning. Once we have identified the priorities, we can begin the task of perfecting man in the cognitive, creative, kinesthetic, and social aspects of his being. We can also demonstrate conclusively that children have made observable and measurable progress in these areas of human growth and development.

Acknowledgments

I want to thank the following persons who read and commented on the manuscript: Dorothy Blackmore, Bessie Frank, L. Frank Mann, Douglas L. Minnis, Margaret M. Nearing, and Richard L. Trapp. I owe a special debt of gratitude to Dr. Blackmore for critical comments and enthusiastic endorsement throughout the writing of this book. Stenographic work was done in a most exemplary manner by Edie Kauffman.

Chapter 9 on Health was written by Dr. John T. Fodor, Professor, Department of Health Science, San Fernando Valley State College.

The understanding and encouragement of my wife, Jeanne, and of my sons, Bruce and Glenn, helped to make the writing of this book a joyful experience.

Contents

The Language of Objectives

Use of Behavioral Objectives

Sources of Objectives

Types of Objectives

Behavioral Objectives offers a practical approach to the improvement of teaching and learning. Teachers benefit by having measurable and observable objectives that are useful in prescribing learning experiences and in evaluating pupil progress. Students benefit by knowing exactly what is expected of them in acquiring knowledge and skills, and through being fully apprised of criteria by which their performance will be judged. This book is not a plea for stripping artistry and compassion from teaching. It deals with a tool which, if wisely used, can facilitate optimum development for the student.

The main object of the educational process is the improvement of student performance; and among the many goals involved in this process are those that relate to the kinds of learning behavior termed *cognitive, affective,* and *psychomotor* (described later in this book). To accomplish any goal, it is desirable to have a clear description or outline of the particular objectives that must be met along the way. For teachers to work successfully in the realm of student performance and achievement, such a description is particularly important — in fact, vital.

We might begin our study of behavioral objectives by indicating what the reader should gain from reading this text. After having read this book and completed the suggested review activity, the reader should be able to:

1. Distinguish between behavioral and non-behavioral goals
2. Determine whether or not goals contain a description of observable or measurable behavior
3. Decide which goals contain proficiency levels or standards for behavior
4. Write behavioral objectives
5. Apply knowledge of behavioral objectives in assessing and improving (a) instructional materials, (b) program, class, and learner objectives, and (c) strategies of teaching

The Language of Objectives

An objective can be defined as an aim or a desirable outcome of action. We use it first to direct our effort and then as a yardstick to assess our degree of achievement—how successful we have been in our effort. In this context, the objective is useful in proportion, first, to how specific it is and, second, to how well we can see or measure its attainment.

Frequently the words *goal* and *objective* are used interchangeably and, to some extent, they are used that way in this text. This is understandable, because each is usually incorporated into definitions of the other. In this book, however, a goal is generally referred to as a general or long-range target or aim, and an objective as a more specific, often short-range statement of intent. A practical resolution of this matter can be seen in two definitions proposed by the California School Boards Association:

Goals.

A goal is a statement that proposes desired and valued competencies, states of being, and/or general levels of proficiency to be achieved. Goals are achieved through the accomplishment of objectives within an educational entity. (Entity may, in this case, refer to a unified, high school, or elementary district, or a school building or classroom.)

Objectives.

An objective is defined as a quantifiable and/or observable achievement accomplished under specifiable conditions. Objectives should reflect the critical factors required for the accomplishment of a goal.[1]

In this book the terms *behavior* and *performance* are used interchangeably. They refer to effort and its results—effort that can be observed or measured, and results that can be judged by measuring or rating.

In judging performance, a standard or criterion is required, and some sort of rating method based on that standard is applied. In this text, the phrase *level of proficiency* is used to indicate a student's standing in relation to the desired performance, or behavior: the results of his efforts are used to determine what that level is. Other terms necessary for the discussion of behavioral objectives are defined within the context of this book.

1. California School Boards Association, *Educational Goals and Objectives* (Sacramento: CSBA, September 1969), pp. 4–5.

Teachers who are most effective in improving the behaviors of pupils are adept at assessing each pupil's uniqueness, preparing assignments and programs for individual learners, setting the stage for learning, and monitoring improvement in individual performance. Behavioral objectives can be instrumental in producing this kind of effective teaching. As expectancies, they can formulate and channel activity, so that they are useful tools for guiding and improving both teaching and learning. Those objectives that are of the greatest value not only describe the *behavior* sought, but also identify expected levels of *proficiency*, mediating *conditions*, and *methods* for assessing whether or not the expected level of proficiency has been attained.

Use of Behavioral Objectives

The formulation of behavioral objectives is an important aspect of all areas of educational planning: curriculum development; course, unit, and lesson planning; selection of instructional materials; choice of teaching methods or strategies; and preparation or selection of tests relevant to the objectives of instruction. Objectives of this type contain measurable or observable indices of performance. Without these it is extremely difficult to make accurate judgments about such planning or to determine whether general educational goals, course objectives, or assignment objectives have been reached.

In addition, behavioral objectives are of immense value in the classroom: if they are framed in a manner that captures the essence rather than the incidental or trivial aspects of learning, and if adroitly employed, they provide a rational and valid basis for directing and assessing the performance of individual students. In *Preparing Instructional Objectives,* Mager asserts, ". . . an instructor will function in a fog of his own making until he knows just what he wants his students to be able to do at the end of the instruction."[2] Mager also makes a valid point in distinguishing between course descriptions (what a course is about) and course objectives (what students should be able to do after completing a course). Indeed, if we are not careful, we can talk on and on about the general aims and content of a course without ever indicating what it is that the teacher and student will do and how the course will result in any observable or measurable progress or improvement.

2. Robert F. Mager, *Preparing Instructional Objectives* (Palo Alto, California: Fearon, 1962), p. 3.

The discipline provided by course objectives will improve the instructional process in any classroom organization. In the heterogeneously grouped class, use of behavioral objectives leads to greater individualization of instruction; it helps program individual students through certain experiences in light of their objectives and needs. Use of such a tool may lead to development of learner-based curriculum, learner-based teaching methodologies, skillful diagnosis and prescription, and open-end curricula—all attributes of continuous progress education. In classes where children are grouped on the basis of maturation, interest, or level of sophistication, the teacher can use behavioral objectives to guide groups of individuals or the whole class through progressive sequences of fact, concept, and skill acquisition.

An important aspect of both heterogeneous and specially grouped classes is pupil-teacher planning, in which pupil and teacher together formulate behavioral objectives. This activity is a worthwhile one through which pupils can gain a greater appreciation for their capabilities. In time, pupils may become capable of formulating their own performance objectives independently, in terms of what they think they can accomplish.

Sources of Objectives

Ideally, educational objectives result from and should represent the synthesis of those ideas most conducive to the best possible development of individuals and to the improvement of society. Such productive ideas can be found in or developed from sources dealing with individual, group, and cultural conditions: in the literature describing or analyzing the goals of education; in publications dealing with national, political, or economic goals; in authoritative material describing children's characteristics and needs; and in the findings of developmental psychology. Another invaluable source is the publication that presents taxonomic structures (conceptualized hierarchical frameworks) of goals and objectives, and that incorporates descriptions of intellectual, creative, affective, and motor skills and abilities. Because objectives should be derived from organized bodies of knowledge, school textbooks themselves are a helpful source, since we presume that they emphasize the basic principles of different areas of knowledge.

It is sometimes difficult to find uniform definition and substantiation of behavioral objectives. Research on educational objectives reveals: a wide disparity in the use of terms; value-laden (affective) phraseology that appears to defy measurement, monitoring, evaluation, and accountability; and few statements of objectives that are substantiated by or formulated as a result of valid and reliable empirical studies.[3] Nevertheless, the usefulness of behavioral objectives continues to generate interest; people in education are not content merely to adopt objectives and goals judged most appropriate by eminent educators and politicians. Teachers, consultants, administrative leaders, school board members, and members of the lay community are now demanding a convincing rationale for educational activities. They also want conceptual tools for determining whether or not the learner has improved in the extent of his knowledge, the degree of his skills, and the expression of his interests and attitudes. Behavioral objectives can serve these purposes.

Before dealing specifically with this type of conceptual tool, it may be helpful to describe and to some degree consider the value of several types of objectives.

Types of Objectives

General and Specific Objectives

College professors and authors of textbooks on education often refer to "general" and "specific" objectives of instruction. General objectives tend to reflect a theme or a concern that applies to education in general or to an abstract reason for offering a particular course or subject. For example, a general objective of a course might be "to help children become familiar with famous works of art"; or "to help pupils gain an appreciation of scientific discovery in the eighteenth century"; or "to develop pupils' understanding of the contributions of minority groups to the culture of the United States."

General objectives such as these are of value in describing what we intend to accomplish. A set of these objectives may be used to define and establish a universe of concern or of attention. Incorporated into school board policy, they provide both general direction and some latitude for innovation in adjusting performance or operations to changing conditions. However, when this type of objective is incorporated into speeches, bulletins, and curriculum guides, parents and teachers alike may wonder what we actually intend. For

3. Margaret Ammons, "Objectives and Outcomes," *Encyclopedia of Educational Research,* 4th ed. (New York: Collier Macmillan Ltd., 1965).

example, "to become a good citizen" and "to achieve economic competence" are heralded goals of education. But
what do we actually mean by "good citizen" and "economic
competence"?

General objectives enhance communication only when
persons in the group for whom they are intended translate such
objectives into approximately the same specific objectives.
For example, does the phrase, "to become a good citizen,"
communicate meaning that is useful for guiding learning? It
does so only when the meaning of the term *good citizen* is
similarly perceived by most of the audience. Obviously, a
large and diversified audience might produce any number of
seemingly incompatible definitions of such a complex term.

Some valid general objectives are: (1) to help each child
become more rational, more creative, and more humane;
(2) to develop within all children a sense of personal worth;
(3) to encourage children to learn how to learn; (4) to foster
within children an enjoyment and an appreciation of art and
music. Other examples of general objectives for students are:
(1) to appreciate the effort expended in building the Empire
State Building in New York and the pyramids in Egypt; (2) to
understand the basic causes of social unrest; (3) to know the
influence of former Chief Justice John Marshall upon the
Supreme Court; and (4) to feel a sense of participation by
being a member of an all-city grade school band. These
general objectives can be readily translated into meaningful
specific objectives.

Specific objectives are those that tend to direct student
activity toward acquiring clearly described traits, attitudes,
skills, and knowledge. They may or may not be behavioral in
nature. Examples of specific objectives are:

1. At the end of this course, the student is to know fifteen
   rights of American citizens.
2. The student is to understand the influence of Thomas
   Wolfe upon other American novelists.
3. Using diagrams which he has made, the pupil is to describe
   five scientific inventions credited to each of three European
   scientists who lived in the eighteenth century.
4. Given a tire jack and a spare tire mounted on a wheel, the
   student is to change a flat tire within ten minutes.
5. When given money and asked to go to the grocery store
   for a quart of milk, the pupil will return with the milk
   within an agreed-upon time and not appropriate any of the
   change.

Even greater progress toward specificity is possible when we
replace nebulous verbs such as *to know* and *to understand*

with verbs that identify observable or measurable performance. Objectives (1) and (2) above then become:

1. At the end of this course, the student will be able to list fifteen rights of an American citizen.
2. The student will document with ten references the contributions of English poets to American literary criticism.

Non-Behavioral and Behavioral Objectives

Moving from the general and specific categories, we might also classify objectives as *non-behavioral* or *behavioral*. Behavioral objectives deal with concrete, specific, measurable goals, whereas the non-behavioral deal with more abstract concepts — philosophic, ideological, attitudinal — which can't easily be measured. To distinguish one kind of goal from the other, we can ask two questions:

1. Is the objective concerned with particular, observable, measurable improvement in student behavior?
2. Does the objective establish a minimal level of proficiency for judging whether or not the behavior has been attained to the degree sought?

Further delineation of a behavioral objective is possible by stating the mediating conditions (facilitating or inhibiting) under which the behavior is to be carried out. In addition, the statements of some behavioral objectives may also include the methods or procedures to be used in observing or measuring the attainment of certain levels of proficiency.

Behavioral objectives are tools that, if used with competence, can do much to improve teaching and learning. They are not in and of themselves better than non-behavioral objectives — any more than specific objectives are more important than general ones. Each type of objective has its own place and contributes to the enhancement of learning. To illustrate, who would say that it is more important to add a column of six five-digit figures in two minutes — a behavioral goal — than to be honest and reliable — a non-behavioral goal? Under most circumstances, it would seem more important to be honest and reliable, a goal which becomes more meaningful when translated into observable and measurable functions. This translation is necessary if objectives are to be of diagnostic, prescriptive, and evaluative value in directing and assessing learning.

The categories of objectives described — general and specific, behavioral or non-behavioral — are obviously not mutually exclusive, but in practice a behavioral objective is used as a type of specific objective, while general objectives are usually non-behavioral statements.

Learning and Teaching Objectives

One pitfall to be avoided in preparing behavioral objectives for the learner is that of inadvertently stating objectives for the teacher. Statements should be in terms of what *the learner* is to be able to do as a result of instruction, starting with the learner and his need to modify his behavior.

Individual and Group Objectives

Individual and group objectives both have their place in guiding and evaluating learning, and the competent teacher is able to accomplish both. The mistake to be avoided is that of using a group objective for directing the activities of all individuals in a group. In the same way, evaluation of group performance is inadequate as a measure of individual performance.

Average levels of performance can be particularly misleading, because they are often skewed by various factors. Instead of beginning a behavioral objective with "The class is to . . .", one might state, "Each pupil in the class is to . . ." or "Pupils who have achieved X level of proficiency are to . . ." It is relatively easy to transform individual learner objectives into group ones by adding indices of group achievement such as "The average score on the range of scores of the class will be . . ."

Following this brief overview of different types of objectives will be a closer look at components of behavioral objectives and steps which can be taken in preparing them.

CHAPTER 1

BEHAVIORAL OBJECTIVES

1

Academic Skills

Higher Cognitive Skills

Creative Skills

Craftsmanship Skills

Leadership Skills

Coding Objectives

Framing Objectives

Professional educators have always been deeply concerned with student performance. Their interest in behavioral objectives as a means of producing the best possible classroom achievement is far from new: it is not merely a response to today's interest in accountability. Educators have always recognized that clear directions must be established for the learner and that he must know, before he begins a task, the standards by which his performance will be judged.

As described earlier, behavioral objectives are intentions, expectancies, or aims that lead us to behave or perform in certain ways. They are useful pedagogical tools because they make it possible to be more precise, logical, and effective in planning and evaluating learning experiences.

What are the characteristics of well-formulated behavioral objectives? First, they are stated in precise language and define the desired behavior clearly. Next, they establish proficiency levels for this behavior that are observable or measurable. In doing so, it may be either necessary or desirable to describe the behavior in some detail, using qualifying phrases or statements that describe conditions under which the terminal behavior will be observed, tested, or judged. Finally, behavioral objectives may also describe procedures for determining whether or not the student can perform at an established level of proficiency.

In writing objectives, teachers should avoid words and phrases that are subject to many definitions, such as *to know, to appreciate, to be familiar with, to enjoy,* and *to understand.* These words and phrases are acceptable in statements of general goals. But unless they are defined distinctly in behavioral terms, they can be of little use in directing and evaluating student performance. It is recommended that teachers, in first working out their objectives, avoid nebulous terms completely, and use only words that deal directly with observable and measurable behavior. To identify the intended behavior clearly, we should use specific verbs of action such as *to identify, to record, to list, to construct, to speak, to write, to solve,* or *to compare.* In addition, certain more abstract intellectual skills may be listed, as long as the desired action is clear: *to analyze, to synthesize, to translate,* or *to evaluate.*

Levels of proficiency must next be included in the behavioral statement. These can be described by listing the desired speed of completion, degree of skill to be developed, or number of items to be produced. At a most rudimentary level, the mere fact that a person walks, talks, or writes a sentence may indicate acceptable levels of proficiency — observable and measurable skills. In going into detail in the description of the objective, the mediating conditions that are given may be facilitating or inhibiting in nature. Some phrases used to describe these types of mediation are: *given, with the aid of, without the use of, in the absence of,* and *under these circumstances.*

If procedures are included for determining whether or not levels of proficiency have been attained, they can vary from observation by a skilled observer to measurement by extremely precise instruments. Two examples of behavioral objectives incorporating such methods are:

1. Following three months of intensive training, the best breast-stroke swimmer on the high-school swimming team is to develop form and speed, using a butterfly breast stroke with a dolphin kick, that should qualify him for first or second place in a statewide competition. This determination will be made *through observation* by a swimming coach who has participated both as a contestant and as a judge in statewide meets.

2. Using a metal lathe, the student is to turn a metal rod until it meets the tolerance standards established by the teacher and determined *by use of a micrometer.*

The five-way classification of behavioral objectives in this book includes those objectives that foster improvement in *academic* or particular subject-matter skills; those that direct activities toward improving specific *cognitive* or thinking skills; those that emphasize *creative* skills; those that highlight *craftsmanship* or kinesthetic skills; and those that emphasize *leadership* skills. The content of this book has been designed to guide the reader in preparing behavioral objectives in each of these five areas.

Academic Skills

Academic studies are defined as those conducted at institutions of higher education; they are not vocational or applied, and may be formal or theoretical. They are considered to fall in the fields of literature and the English language, history, the behavioral sciences, the physical and biological sciences, mathematics, fine arts, and philosophy.

Up to the present time, the main emphasis in general education has been upon the acquisition of knowledge, and the educational process was primarily one in which information and ideas were presented to the student, whose main task was to retain them. Today high schools, colleges, and universities are reshaping their curricula to help develop other and "higher" intellectual skills as well as creative attitudes and behaviors. With this change and with increased interaction between "the world" and the university, a new definition of the word *academic* may be evolved, a definition that in time might encompass objectives, programs, activities, and functions that would perceive and develop man in all aspects of his being.[1]

Examples of Academic Behavioral Objectives

English and Literature

1. Each sixth-grade student is to write a theme, consisting of three one-hundred word paragraphs, in which the first sentence in each paragraph either introduces the topic of the paragraph or provides a transition from the previous paragraph.
2. Each student is to match with no more than one error four poets and poems studied by the class.

Social Sciences

1. After a study of their community, third-grade pupils are to give verbal directions that would guide visitors from pupil's homes to the principal's office, the nearest mailbox, the nearest fire station, a restaurant, and a drug store.
2. Twelfth-grade students are to describe in a 500-word paper methods of investigation or research used by five different types of social scientists.

---

1. Paul D. Plowman, "Encouraging the Development of the Talented — In Academic Areas," adapted from the September–October, 1967, issue of EDUCATION. Copyright, 1967, by The Bobbs-Merrill Company, Inc., Indianapolis, Indiana.

Science

Using the appropriate formula, a stop watch, and a weight, students in a physics class are to calculate within three feet the height of a three-story building. Accuracy is to be determined by comparing the calculations with the official specifications on approved architectural plans.

Health

After a study of health in the home and at school, each second-grade pupil is to draw a picture illustrating a basic rule of good health. To complete this assignment or objective satisfactorily, at least three classmates must identify the rule illustrated in the picture. The child drawing each picture must be able to explain verbally what he drew.

Mathematics

1. Third-grade pupils are to be able to read and write accurately any number from 1 to 10,000. This is to be done following instruction and practice in writing such numbers and in a manner meriting a satisfactory rating by the teacher.
2. Eighth-grade students calculate how far they are from a thunderstorm when they hear thunder three seconds after they see a flash of lightning. The calculations are to be judged accurate enough approximations by the teacher.
3. Bar graphs, circle graphs, and line graphs are to be constructed and a paragraph written indicating when each type is best used. Graph usage and construction are to be substantiated by a notebook with clippings that illustrate how businesses and governmental agencies use each of these ways of presenting information.

Reading

1. Upon entering third grade, pupils in the top reading group are to identify by sight with no errors each word on a published word test.
2. After participating in fifteen one-hour periods of instruction and drill in skimming, scanning, and comprehension skills, each tenth-grade student is to increase his effective reading rate by 200 percent.

Art and Music

1. Eighth-grade students are to be able to identify the following art elements in six paintings: negative and positive areas, perspective, balance, value, and rhythm.

2. As a result of having taken a music appreciation course, and after listening to recorded selections of ten symphonies, the student is to identify the composer of each symphony.
3. The third-grade student is to identify the instrument when hearing solos played with a cello, clarinet, trombone, oboe, and bassoon.

Cognitive Skills

In considering the development of cognitive, or thinking, skills, two publications that present powerful educational concepts are particularly recommended: the *Taxonomy of Educational Objectives, Handbook I: Cognitive Domain,* and Guilford's "The Structure of the Intellect." The "cognitive domain" of the *Taxonomy* analyzes thinking skills in the categories of remembering, comprehending, applying, analyzing, synthesizing, and evaluating knowledge.[2] In "The Structure of the Intellect" Guilford advances the categories of cognitive ability, memory, convergent thinking, divergent thinking, and evaluative ability.[3]

We use the word *taxonomy* to mean an orderly classification of objectives, principles, and facts according to their natural and logical relationships. In dealing with educational objectives, such a system is considered preferable to one that imposes arbitrary classifications upon behaviors without regard to their actual and natural relationships. The *Taxonomy* illustrates a natural organization, providing six major classes of behavior: (1) Knowledge, (2) Comprehension, (3) Application, (4) Analysis, (5) Synthesis, and (6) Evaluation. The behaviors in each class are likely to use and be built on the behaviors found in the preceding class. The first or lowest level, knowledge (which mainly involves remembering), provides a basis for the next level, comprehension, with its skills of interpretation, translation, and extrapolation. Comprehension in turn is needed before knowledge can be applied (the third level), and the operations of analysis, synthesis, and evaluation can be performed.

Thorough comprehension of the "Cognitive Domain" may seem to be an extremely difficult task. The authors do not

2. See Benjamin Bloom and David R. Krathwohl, *Taxonomy of Educational Objectives, Handbook I: Cognitive Domain* (New York: David McKay Company, Inc., 1956).

3. See J. P. Guilford, "Creativity: Its Measurement and Development," in *A Source Book for Creative Thinking,* eds. Sidney J. Parnes and Harold F. Harding (New York: Charles Scribner's Sons, 1962).

suggest that it be read in one sitting. Instead, they advise the reader to mull over the structure, the categories, and the ideas for applying it in improving instruction. Interpretive and translative publications which may be helpful include "An Interpretation of the *Taxonomy of Educational Objectives*" by the author, and *Classroom Questions—What Kinds?* by Norris Sanders.

To acquaint themselves with this taxonomic approach to ordering skills and objectives, teachers can practice framing behavioral questions that fit at each level; they can also analyze examination or study questions, classroom dialogue, and curriculum materials on the basis of the *Taxonomy*. Following is an overview of the taxonomic levels, with examples of appropriate behavioral objectives.

Knowledge Level

The knowledge level is primarily one of remembering — remembering an idea, a phenomenon, or a fact. A behavioral objective at this level might be:

> Having taken an American Red Cross first-aid course, the student will identify pictures of the three types of burns and explain approved first-aid treatment for each type of burn. His identification and explanation are to match those in the Red Cross First-Aid Manual.

Comprehension Level

Translation, interpretation, and extrapolation are elements of comprehension.

Translation. The cognitive process of translation involves taking an idea or event and communicating it in a new form. This can be done by changing a written or spoken statement into another language or mathematical formula, or by saying something in one's own words. Translation may mean moving from the concrete to the abstract or from the abstract to the concrete in expressing an idea. Two examples of behavioral objectives are:

1. Within a fifty-five minute period, the high-school student will summarize in a written composition in German the philosophy underlying the American Declaration of Independence. His proficiency in this task will be judged "acceptable" by a member of a high-school or college German Department.

2. The student will look at a plan of the family living quarters in a low-cost housing project, a condominium, and a real estate developer's portrayal of a modern home. He will

choose a room from any of these plans and prepare a written statement containing the same information intended by the symbols and lines. That the statements contain the same information will be certified by a member of the American Institute of Architects.

Interpretation. Interpretation, another skill involved in comprehension, means seeing relationships among events, ideas, or social, political, economic, or physical structures. It may also mean rearranging or reordering ideas and perceiving these as they relate to one's own background of ideas and experiences. Examples of behavioral objectives are:

1. Given three standard textbooks on high-school chemistry, the student will read appropriate sections and then explain why the formula for water may be written as HOH or H_2O. This interpretation will be verified as accurate from sections in these textbooks.
2. After studying time-lapse photographs of the development of a flower from a seed, a child will write a paragraph interpreting what happened. The child's interpretation will be considered adequate if the basic facts presented are consistent with scientific explanations appearing in a botany textbook.

Extrapolation. Extrapolation is an intellectual skill that takes one beyond translation and interpretation to a projection of the effects of certain behaviors or conditions. Examples of behavioral objectives are:

1. Upon hearing a story about an injury to a pet, a primary child is to say what might happen to him if he, too, should run across the street without looking.
2. After a thorough study of each of the rights listed in the Bill of Rights, including the reasons for incorporating them into the U.S. Constitution, eighth-grade students are to write 750-word essays on the topic, "What life might be like in the United States today if the Bill of Rights had not become part of the U.S. Constitution."

Teachers and administrators might wish to extrapolate from the following: How might teaching and school administration change if we accept the following principles? (1) The central purpose of American education is to help man become more rational.[4] (2) A person is rational to the extent that he uses all available data in solving problems and to the extent that he considers all possible solutions.

---

4. See National Education Association, Educational Policies Commission, *The Central Purpose of American Education* (Washington, D.C.: 1961).

Application Level

At the application level of cognition, the student applies learned principles to new situations, or uses information from various sources or subject areas to solve a problem. Behavioral objectives emphasizing this level of thinking are:

1. After studying principles of buoyancy during a fifth- or sixth-grade science class, students will demonstrate these principles with pieces of wood, cork, Styrofoam, air-filled bottles and plastic bags, and lead weights.
2. Twelfth-grade students are to read three references on principles of conservation and then to apply these principles to social relations by writing a theme on the topic, "How Americans might use knowledge of conservation principles in solving or ameliorating racial problems and tensions." The suggested application of these principles is to be judged creative and feasible by a panel of three students and two teachers.

Analysis Level

Analysis is the process of separating into component parts a whole such as a mathematical or social problem, a painting, or a scientific phenomenon or object. As a cognitive skill, it enables us to determine characteristics of such things as human organisms or chemical reactions. It helps us to explain why things are as they are or why they behave as they do. Examples of behavioral objectives at this level are:

1. Upon completing inquiry training, and after applying inquiry techniques to explain certain discrepant events in science, the student examines a problem, such as that of persons living in poverty in an affluent society, shown in study prints, a filmstrip, or a film. He is then to list five causes of the problem or break a general problem down into a series of at least three specific problems that need to be resolved in order to resolve the general one.
2. The pupil is to use his senses of touch, sight, and taste to identify correctly five out of ten unknown substances.

Synthesis Level

Synthesis is the process of putting together parts or elements to form a whole; in the cognitive domain, it can be considered the category involving the most creative behavior on the part of the learner. Creativity enters into other cognitive levels, of course (though knowledge, the first level, must be considered prerequisite to other, more creative levels): comprehension includes playing with ideas at the extrapolation level; application involves putting criteria, principles, and data to use in new situations; and analysis may isolate components and thereby make possible new relationships and products. However, these levels involve creativity only in part, whereas synthesis calls for a totality of creative behavior. Examples of behavioral objectives at the synthesis level are:

1. The eighth-grade student is to make a half-hour multimedia presentation of the topic, "What youth could do to help other people, themselves, and their country." The audio-visual media will include a tape recorder, an overlay projector, and a colored-slide projector. The tape recorder will be used to present appropriate selections of modern poetry or prose; the overhead projector will project various combinations of color (through color pigments mixed with water in a glass pie plate); and the colored-slide projector will show a presentation of youths helping other people, themselves, and their country.
2. To demonstrate his verbal fluency, the sixth-grade student is to write a story using in order each of fifteen unrelated words listed by the teacher. Four out of five students who read the story are to rate it as understandable and original.

Evaluation Level

Evaluation is the cognitive skill of appraising and making judgments about the value of ideas, objects, or conditions. Judgments are made on the basis of standards and criteria given to the student, or on criteria based on his internal values. Evaluation involves some aspects of all the other cognitive levels, but adds the aspect of value. Examples of behavioral objectives at this level are:

1. After reading in *Hamlet* the advice of Polonius to his son, Laertes, the student is to say which aspects of that advice are applicable today.
2. Each member of an eleventh-grade class is to rate the behavior of each character in a novel by (a) the virtue checklist which Benjamin Franklin published in his autobiography, (b) the "Ten Commandments," or (c) the elements of a personal code which he himself has developed.

From the above examples, we can see that the *Taxonomy* may be used as a basis for a systematic approach to the development of better teaching and learning experiences, including classroom dialog and assignments. Other systems could also be constructed, presenting hierarchical structures or specific objectives and establishing levels of competence. Beside being used to determine students' proficiency, they can be immensely valuable in appraising students' cognitive skills and discovering new methods and resources for developing them.

Creative Skills

To create is essentially to bring something into existence for the first time — something new or without precedent. Creativity, the attitude or process that brings this about, extends awareness, overcomes obstacles to thinking and doing, and engenders original and admirable products. Students can gain insight and become more sensitive in understanding concepts and dealing with problems if objectives are planned to develop their creative skills and attitudes. Some examples of behavioral objectives emphasizing creative skills are:

1. After instruction and practice in the four steps of the creative process described by Wallas (preparation, incubation, illumination, and revision),[5] each student will indicate that, by applying these steps, he is able to generate at least fifty percent more solutions to problems than when he did not apply creative process strategy. Using criteria agreed upon by the students, a panel of students is to judge that, by following a creative-process strategy, the student not only came up with more alternatives, but that there was improvement in the quality of the proposed solutions.

2. Middle-class suburban children are to list (a) what they consider to be the three most pressing problems of our society, and (b) solutions which they propose to solve the problems, first as a classroom assignment; second, after spending one day touring a ghetto area in a large city; and third, after spending two weeks during a summer vacation building a recreation center together with children from a ghetto. A comparison of responses made at each of the three stages is to show that students changed their responses after the one-day trip, and to a greater degree after the summer work program.

3. Following a semester of exploring a variety of media, in which the traits and processes of creativity are discussed, and after participating in three ten-minute divergent-thinking sessions, three out of ten students are to design three-dimensional art objects that are judged original by a panel of four artists.

5. See Graham Wallas, *The Art of Thought* (New York: Harcourt, Brace & World, 1926).

4. Using a checklist of idea-generating questions,[6] each student will state three ways of putting pliers to new uses; three ways of improving two home appliances by minimizing or rearranging components; and ten ways of improving instruction by modifying teacher and pupil roles and expectations.

Craftsmanship Skills

Specific kinesthetic-skill objectives will, of course, vary from craft to craft. However, craftsmanship in a general sense might imply:

1. Preparing a reasonable plan
2. Selecting appropriate tools
3. Choosing proper materials
4. Applying tools skillfully in making a useful, beautiful, accurate, or worthwhile product

Behavioral objectives should specify in performance terms what is meant by *reasonable, appropriate, proper, skillfully, useful, accurate,* and *worthwhile.* Examples of craftsmanship behavioral objectives are:

1. Girls in a seventh-grade home economics class are to select from a set of tools the appropriate scissors for cutting heavy woolen fabric and for cutting thread. The standards for what is most appropriate will be those mentioned in their seventh-grade homemaking textbook.
2. Each fifth-grade boy will carve an Indian canoe from a large block of soap in a period of twenty minutes.

Leadership Skills

Leadership skills are those that show ability to engage in an activity or to see that tasks are carried out efficiently, with a minimum of interruption and indecision. In addition to skill in motivation, the skill of leadership involves the ability to plan activities (including preparing performance objectives); skill in organizing and coordinating efforts of other persons; skill in protecting individual members of a group; and skill in evaluating the functioning of the group, the functioning of

6. See John E. Arnold, "Useful Creative Techniques" in *A Source Book for Creative Teaching* (New York: Charles Scribner's Sons, 1962), p. 254.

individuals, and the results of the group effort. Examples of leadership behavioral objectives follow:

1. After five sixth-grade students have had one week of instruction and practice in leadership, each is to organize and direct a twenty-minute activity for a group of five persons in such a manner that (a) group members use resources around the room without disturbing other students; (b) it is not necessary for the teacher to intervene and direct the group; and (c) three out of the four tasks assigned by the teacher or group leader at the beginning of the period are completed to the satisfaction of the group members, the group chairman, and the teacher.

2. Following a series of three filmed presentations and practice drills, each tenth-grade student in a class on first aid and fire safety will escort ten second-grade children 100 feet in single file onto the playground during a fire drill. This will be done with no verbal directions or gestures by teachers or school administrators.

We have presented here an overview of five categories of behavioral objectives — academic, cognitive, creative, craftmanship, and leadership. It should, of course, be recognized that other sets of categories or structures of objectives may be equally as valid. Notable among these are the "Affective Domain" of the *Taxonomy of Educational Objectives;*[7] a psychomotor domain; and, yet to be formulated, a "unified-field" structure of objectives for optimum development of human beings.

It should also be noted that categories of behavioral objectives cannot be treated as entirely separate from each other; they overlap quite naturally at certain points. This is particularly evident in the intimate relationship among some traits of creativity and certain higher cognitive skills. Efforts to extend human awareness, sensitivity, flexibility, and fluency in thought, and the ability to toy with a whole range of ideas, have a very direct impact on man's rationality and functioning intelligence. A key mark of rationality and intelligence is one's ability to consider facts from a number of areas in solving problems and to consider all possible (or at least an optimum number of) alternatives in making a decision or in solving a problem. Productive divergent thinking is, indeed, an earmark of human intelligence. In addition, hierarchical structures, for example, the "Cognitive Domain" of the

7. David R. Krathwohl, Benjamin Bloom, and B. B. Masia, *Taxonomy of Educational Objectives — Handbook II: Affective Domain* (New York: David McKay Company, Inc., 1956).

Taxonomy, may be cumulative in nature—with aspects of lower-level categories of objectives actually forming part of higher-level objectives. An example in point is the knowledge base necessary for comprehension, the next higher level.

Coding Objectives

Coding is a simple analytic method for identifying the key components of written behavioral objectives, e.g., behavior, mediating conditions, level of proficiency, or assessment methods. One way to code is to use different-colored pencils or pens to notate which characteristics are included in a statement. Another method might be to assign a code letter to each characteristic, and then record in the margin the code letters for those characteristics that appear in the statement.

Coding can be an excellent way of learning to identify the key elements of objectives, and as a pedagogical method it has a useful place in in-service and teacher-training programs. It is also valuable for evaluating school district plans and objectives, as well as those that appear in textbooks, teaching guides, and curriculum guides. If this analysis shows that certain objectives do not describe observable or measurable behavior or expected levels of proficiency, a decision would have to be made whether or not to supplement existing general or non-behavioral objectives with objectives that are specific and behavioral. Remember that as indications of intent, general objectives do have their place. Behavioral objectives, on the other hand, are needed as specific guidelines to the learner.

Coding designations used in this book are:

B—a clear description of *Behavior*

C—mediating *Conditions*

P—level of *Proficiency*

M—*Methods* for ascertaining that the proficiency level has been reached

Review

Using the code designations, *B, C, P,* and *M,* indicate which elements are present in the following statements:

___1. After listening to a recording of the inaugural address of John F. Kennedy, the student lists three things that the late President said.

___2. Students are to appreciate poetry.

___3. Skills of oral presentation are to be perfected by the student until he wins a debate sponsored by the National Forensic League.

___4. Pupils are to learn the significance of the Declaration of Independence by observing and discussing a play on Colonial America.

___5. Without the aid of a dictionary, the pupil is to write correctly the spelling of five words dictated by the teacher.

Which of the above statements are behavioral objectives, containing a clear description of behavior (B) and a specified level of proficiency (P)? Which do not contain any of the characteristics of a behavioral objective? Which contain all four characteristics? Answers appear on page 20.

At this point, you may want to practice coding additional objectives, using those in other books or those previously given as examples in different subject areas. After this experience in coding, you will be ready to consider steps in framing objectives.

Framing Objectives

Four specific steps serve as a guideline for framing behavioral objectives.

1. Make a clear, precise determination of what it is you want the learner to do.
2. Establish both the limiting and facilitating conditions under which the learner is to do what is asked.
3. Define the minimally acceptable level of proficiency.
4. Decide what methods to use in judging whether or not a student is behaving at the established level(s) of proficiency.

Persons learning to prepare objectives are advised to follow Steps 1, 2, and 3, and periodically to follow all four steps, although the mere statement of a certain skill or behavior might be considered an adequate though rudimentary level of proficiency. There are times when it will be possible to think of a condition as a standard (proficiency level) and a standard as a condition, because they both modify or describe the behavior. For example, in the objective, "The student is to walk twenty-five miles *during a twelve-hour period*," what is "during a twelve-hour period"? From one perspective, it can be thought of as a condition under which the student is to demonstrate that he can walk twenty-five miles. From another perspective "during a twelve-hour period" can be considered a part of the level of proficiency.

Another suggestion for writing objectives is to experiment with various ways of stating them. There is nothing more tedious than attempting to wade through seemingly endless lists of objectives, all of which begin with, "Given . . ., the learner . . ." Variety may be achieved by beginning statements with:

1. The pupil describes . . .
2. Eight-grade students are to be able to . . .
3. To construct a redwood bench according to specifications . . .
4. Ninety-five percent of the students in the ninth-grade science class . . .

Some persons may take issue with the inclusion of example 4, contending that it is a class rather than a learner objective. In reply, it might be argued that example 4 can be thought of as an individual learner objective if it is immediately translated to refer to each of the students within the 95-percent group. By incorporating group indices of attainment, individual learner objectives may be translated into class, teacher, or program objectives.

Variety in stating conditions may be accomplished by use of such phrases as:

1. Under the following circumstances . . .
2. With the aid of (two other students, a slide rule) . . .
3. Without the aid of (his textbook, the teacher, a blueprint) . . .
4. In the absence of (a school rule to guide his behavior) . . .
5. Confronted with (an accident victim, a rabid dog, an angry group of classmates) . . .
6. Given (paint, lumber) . . .

Variety in writing proficiency levels may be achieved by varying the specifications for time allotted for the behavior, quantity or production, quality of product, or degree of skill. Methods for measuring whether the established level of proficiency has been reached may be standard or non-standard; stop watches, simple counting, standardized rating sheets, and tests are but a few of the means that might be employed.

A card file box and packets of white, green, pink, blue, and beige cards are useful for the exercise suggested in this book. If colored cards are not available, get white ones and color the top edges. The color coding for the cards might be:

1. White — *academic skills*
2. Green — *higher cognitive skills*

3. Pink — *creative skills*
4. Blue — *leadership skills*
5. Beige — *craftsmanship skills*

After preparing behavioral objectives in the various academic fields, file the cards and keep them for ready reference in planning learning experiences for pupils. A system of exchanging behavioral objectives with co-workers might prove helpful.

In a sense, it may be convenient and desirable to obtain prepackaged sets of carefully developed objectives. It should be recognized, though, that however well these may help a pupil move successfully through a sequence of skill development and concept development, it may be necessary to develop specific objectives for him in response to his particular problems or learning needs. For this, the professional teacher is equipped with the skill to develop on-the-spot objectives suitable for guiding and evaluating the work of that individual. If prepared collections do not help, and if the file box of objectives does not cover the situation, then the teacher should be able to create appropriate objectives with the student at the time of need.

Summary of Main Points

1. Teacher success is a product of many factors — antecedents to the learning encounter, the nature of the encounter, and the ability to assess where one started, what one attempted, and what one actually accomplished.

2. Behavioral objects are conceptual tools. Their worth, like the worth of any tool, depends upon how skillfully they are used. One of the primary tasks of the teacher is to determine the anticipated terminal behaviors or performances that specify what he intends and the levels of proficiency, criteria, or standards by which he will measure or judge the results.

3. Persons in the educational profession will not be able to rely for long upon gross measures or group indices of success. They are being asked to demonstrate specifically how, as a result of their efforts, individual children have improved in developing academic, cognitive, creative, craftsmanship, and leadership skills. Assessment and prescription are becoming global functions that necessitate a thorough look at behavioral competencies before and after the teaching-learning act. A key purpose of education is to modify behavior; behavioral objectives are directed toward this end.

4. Helpful in the task of full development of human potential are the skills to prepare behavioral objectives and the means for realizing these objectives. Illustrative objectives in various subject areas, and illustrative cognitive, creative, craftsmanship, and leadership skill objectives have been included in this chapter to give an idea of how behavioral objectives may be a part of a total approach, part of an attempt to improve man in all aspects of his being.

5. To a large extent, the possession of the creative skill to formulate and apply behavioral objectives mark a teacher as a "master" teacher. This appellation may well result in part from parents who are grateful for seeing clearly the earmarks of academic, cognitive, creative, craftsmanship, and leadership competence in their boys and girls. It may come in part from the pupils themselves, who have a clear picture of where they are heading, how they are going to get there, and what they will be like as the result of many fascinating encounters.

Discussion Questions and Activities

Several questions can be posed to assess understandings and skills gained from this chapter and to provide departure points for small-group discussions. The discussions will be most meaningful if participants have access to and study the books referred to on page 21. Some of these books should be part of the teacher's personal library and should be purchased for the school library as well.

Leaders of small groups might proceed through the following questions, taking care to allow full discussion and to assure complete understanding before proceeding from one item to another.

1. What is a behavioral objective? Define this term in your own words.

2. Give two examples of behavioral objectives outside the field of education that direct activity and emphasize performance.

3. Give two examples of behavioral objectives in education.

4. What are the distinguishing features of this kind of objective?

5. Are behavioral objectives more important than non-behavioral objectives? Explain.

6. How might skill in preparing and using behavioral objectives benefit the teacher? The student?

7. The five-way system for classifying behavioral objectives in this book involves academic, cognitive, creative, craftsmanship, and leadership skills. Are these discrete and independent categories? What relationships exist between creative and cognitive skills?

8. List and describe two or more of the following skills.
   a. Academic skills
   b. Cognitive skills
   c. Creative skills
   d. Craftsmanship skills
   e. Leadership skills

9. Write five behavioral objectives for each of the skill areas mentioned in item 8 using the card file system mentioned previously. Each of these should incorporate the first three distinguishing features of behavioral objectives and should be appropriate for students and courses that you are now teaching, have taught, or anticipate teaching.

Answer to Review Questions

Pages 14 and 15:

Elements Present	Elements Not Present
1. B & C & P	M
2.	B P C & M
3. P	B C & M
4. C	B P & M
5. B C P & M	

Bibliography

Alberta Department of Education. *Summary Description of Grade Nine Science Objectives and Test Items.* Edmonton, Alberta: Alberta Department of Education, March 1965.

———. *Summary Description of Grade Nine Social Studies Objectives and Test Items.* Edmonton, Alberta: Alberta Department of Education, January 1966.

Ammerman, Harry L. "Some Important Ways in Which Performance Objectives Can Vary," *Deriving, Specifying, and Using Instructional Objectives,* by William H. Melching et al. Alexandria, Va.: Human Resources Agency of George Washington University, 1966.

Ammons, Margaret. "Objectives and Outcomes," *Encyclopedia of Educational Research,* 4th ed. Edited by Robert Ebel. New York: Crowell Collier & Macmillan, 1965.

Armstrong, Robert J., et al., eds. *Developing and Writing Behavioral Objectives.* Tucson, Ariz.: Educational Innovators Press, 1968.

Arnold, John E. "Useful Creative Techniques," *A Source Book for Creative Thinking.* Edited by Sidney J. Parnes and Harold F. Harding. New York: Scribner's, 1962.

Ayers, J. C. "Developing Descriptions of Objectives and Test Items." Paper read at International Workshop on Possibilities and Limitations of Educational Testing at the International Conference on Educational Testing, May 1967, Berlin.

Baughman, Gerald D., and Mayrhofer, Albert. "Leadership Training Project: A Final Report," *Journal of Secondary Education* 40, no. 8 (December 1965): 369–72.

Bloom, Benjamin, and Krathwohl, David R., *Taxonomy of Educational Objectives,* Handbook I: *Cognitive Domain.* New York: McKay, 1956.

California School Boards Association. *Educational Goals and Objectives.* Sacramento, Calif.: CSBA, September 1969.

Dave, R. H. "Taxonomy of Educational Objectives and Achievement Testing." Paper read at the International Conference on Educational Testing, May 1967, Berlin.

Educational Policies Commission. *The Central Purpose of American Education.* Washington: National Education Association, 1961.

Gronlund, Norman E. *Stating Behavioral Objectives for Classroom Instruction.* Toronto, Ontario: Macmillan, 1970.

Guilford, J. P. "Creativity: Its Measurement and Development," *A Source Book for Creative Thinking.* Edited by Sidney J. Parnes and Harold F. Harding. New York: Scribner's, 1962.

Havighurst, Robert J. *Developmental Tasks and Education.* New York: McKay, 1952.

Instructional Objectives Exchange, Center for the Study of Evaluation. Los Angeles: University of California. (All publications.)

Krathwohl, David R.; Bloom, Benjamin; and Masia, B. B. *Taxonomy of Educational Objectives,* Handbook II: *Affective Domain.* New York: McKay, 1956.

Lessinger, Leon. "Test Building and Test Banks Through the Use of the Taxonomy of Educational Objectives," *California Journal of Educational Research* 14 (November 1963): 195–201.

Mager, Robert R. *Preparing Instructional Objectives.* Palo Alto, California: Fearon, 1962.

Metos, Thomas II, et al. "Developing an American History Test Bank." *Journal of Secondary Education* 41 (March 1966): 105–110.

National Education Association, Educational Policies Commission. 1961. *The Central Purpose of American Education.* Washington.

Plowman, Paul D. "An Interpretation of the *Taxonomy of Educational Objectives.*" Sacramento, Calif.: Paul Plowman, 1968.

Popham, W. James, et al. *Instructional Objectives.* Washington: American Education Research Association, 1969.

Popham, W. James, *The Teacher Empiricist.* Los Angeles: Tinnon-Brown, 1970.

Sanders, Norris M. *Classroom Questions — What Kinds?* New York: Harper & Row, 1966.

Vimcet Filmstrip–Tape Programs. "Educational Objectives," "Establishing Performance Standards," "A Curriculum Rationale," "Defining Content for Objectives," and "Identifying Affect Objectives." Los Angeles: Vimcet Associates, 1967–1969.

Walbesser, Henry H. *Constructing Behavioral Objectives.* College Park, Maryland: Bureau of Educational Research and Field Services, College of Education, University of Maryland, 1968.

Wallas, Graham. *The Art of Thought.* New York: Harcourt, Brace, 1926.

Williams, Frank E. *Workshops on the Use and Adaptation of New Media for Developing Creativity.* St. Paul: Macalester College, 1968.

CHAPTER 2

SEQUENCES OF BEHAVIORAL OBJECTIVES

2

Types of Sequences

Steps in Sequencing Objectives

Examples of Sequences

Learning is a cumulative process. Because of this, performance in any one scholastic area should not be viewed in isolation. Classroom learning should be accomplished through a flow of progressive and reinforcing experiences. The behavioral objectives that direct this learning should reflect this continuity by being integrated into the total curriculum; aside from their individual intent, they should be conceived as sequences. Hopefully, this sequencing will reduce much of the fragmentation of learning and portray the development of concepts and skills as an unfolding drama.

The various kinds of student behavior—such as the five presented in this text—are integrated both potentially and actually, and this is highlighted when objectives are written as sequences. This will reveal not only the degree to which students should acquire concepts and skills, say, in the area of cognition, but also how that one area can lead to a more sophisticated one, or to a complex of them.

This chapter describes a number of different sequences. It also suggests steps educators can take in preparing such progressions of related objectives, and presents examples of different types of sequences as models which readers might use as a basis for preparing their own programed continuums of learning experiences. Since the primary reason for establishing sequences is to facilitate and integrate learning, the following descriptions are presented as ways of organizing the learning of related skills and concepts.

Types of Sequences

Academic-Skill Sequences

In the basic process of learning facts and developing academic skills (such as reading and computing), children should be given a series of steps that are cumulative and that reinforce one another. If instruction is unrelated and fragmented, students may have trouble retaining and using knowledge and skills, and retroactive inhibition may result.

Developmental and Maturative Sequences

Behavioral objective sequences that focus more upon social and psychological behavior are called *maturative and developmental* sequences. They are based upon two sources: 1) the findings of developmental psychologists, who identify progressive sequences of behavior, and 2) methods of delineating tasks that children must perform successfully before becoming recognized members of more advanced maturative groups.

The developmental-psychology approach highlighted in recent years by Jean Piaget proposes that the child be immersed in a host of direct experiences involving all the senses, before attempts are made to develop his abstract thinking, such as his ability to discern the meaning of concepts and symbols.[1] Children progress from knowledge of facts to comprehension of concepts, or from recognition and manipulation of concrete objects to recognition and manipulation of abstract representations of those objects.

Developmental sequences can be constructed in which the key elements are personal-societal tasks.[2] By helping a child perform skills of citizenship or acquire economic independence, teachers can help encourage growth toward social satisfaction, and a feeling of belonging to and of effectively participating in the adult community.[3]

Figure 1 suggests the direction planning such a sequence might take, and illustrates that the use of progressive sequences of behavior overlaps with the delineation of maturative tasks. Sequencing experiences based on developmental tasks may depend both upon relationships that exist among these tasks, and upon the maturation levels toward which the child is striving. For example, one can certainly note relationships that exist between attempting to become economically independent and choosing a career.

Maturative levels might be early childhood, middle childhood, adolescence, and beginning adulthood. Each level can be seen in the following examples. After a child learns how to walk, he can learn how to run. After he learns how to walk and run, he can learn to play a number of games — tennis, football, volleyball, baseball, and basketball. Once a child learns how to read, he can learn now to search a number of printed sources for information. When he has acquired this skill, he

---

1. See Joseph Featherstone, "How Children Learn" (*The New Republic,* August and September 1967).

2. See Robert G. Havighurst, *Developmental Tasks and Education* (New York: McKay, 1952).

3. See Krug, Edward A., *Curriculum Planning* (New York: Harper & Brothers, 1950).

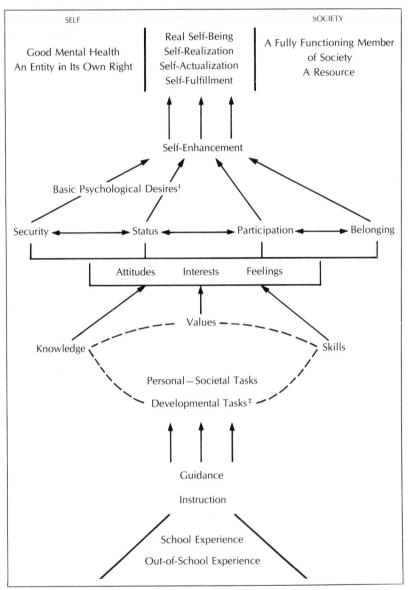

1. See references: Abraham Maslow, Eric Fromm, Victor Frankel, Sidney Jourard.
2. Developmental tasks for the adolescent, for example, would be to become
   emotionally independent of his parents; to acquire a set of values; to form
   a philosophy of life; to acquire skills of citizenship; and to take steps to
   become emotionally independent. See references: Edward Krug, Robert
   Havighurst.

Fig. 1 — Maturative Developmental Sequences— Components

may be able to pursue a number of careers or to matriculate at a college or university. Or, once a child has learned how to plan a work of art and select tools and a medium, he can proceed to create a work of art.

Grade-Level Sequences

A familiar type of sequence is the one which is built to conform to the structured curriculum of the graded school. These have historically been established for administrative convenience. While they are appropriate for most children within the middle ranges of ability, grade-level sequences of knowledge acquisition and skill development may be unreasonably difficult for the slow learner and much too easy for the bright child. Therefore, caution must be exercised in their use.

Cognitive-Skill Sequences

Sequencing the acquisition of cognitive skills is an area of great promise. As already indicated, one basis for this activity, the *Taxonomy of Educational Objectives,* is cumulative in nature (see Figure 2): knowledge must be acquired before it can be fully comprehended through interpretive, extrapolative, and translative skills; in turn, comprehension becomes the basis for efforts at applying, analyzing, synthesizing, and evaluating knowledge. Then new knowledge resulting from evaluation may set the stage for new levels of comprehension, application, analysis, and synthesis.

Guilford's model can be used as another guide in preparing sequences of cognitive objectives, if we allow for the fact that cognition and memory must be developed first. Then

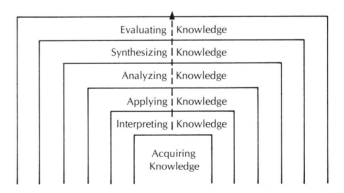

Fig. 2 — Cumulative Sequence — Acquisition of Knowledge to Evaluation

sequences of objectives can be built upon the intellectual operations of divergent production, convergent production, and evaluation. In considering a problem or a question, a number of alternative solutions are generated through divergent thinking; it is then possible to focus upon one and, in a forceful convergent problem-solving manner, to seek an answer or solution. The answer or solution represents a new level of awareness and may start another series of thought. Thus a type of spiraling cyclical sequence resulting from the use of either the *Taxonomy* model or Guilford's model can be visualized.

Learning-Composite Sequences

Another type of sequence is one that is comprised of several areas of educational development. For example, a composite of social science concepts, language arts skills, and maturative-developmental tasks can be used in a series of three-dimensional learning experiences. Figure 3 shows how the three areas might be formulated in this series. Based on this first series, other, more advanced composites could be developed that would noticeably further student growth in sophistication of concepts, comprehension, skills, maturation, and proficiency in developmental tasks. Behavioral objectives must be written for one composite, or a series of them, that would at the same time advance student progress in the three areas of learning.

Programming Development of Creative, Craftsmanship, and Leadership Skills

Sequential learning and behavioral objectives fostering such learning are possible in the areas of creative, craftsmanship, and leadership talent. In a process somewhat akin to the unfolding of a flower, teachers can help persons develop sensitivity and awareness. The creative act of becoming more sensitive and aware may call for new perceptions of one's environment, of one's relationships with other persons, and of one's self. It may mean overcoming perceptual sets and some diffusion of the ego. It may involve developing an awareness of oneself as a person, rather than merely a performer of roles or a player of games dictated by society.

A series of performance objectives designed to promote craftsmanship could involve progression from preparing a plan, to choosing materials, to selecting tools, and finally to applying tools skillfully in creating a product. Growth in the skills of leadership might be noted as a person progresses successfully through a succession of experiences that require proficiency in planning an activity, in directing persons and

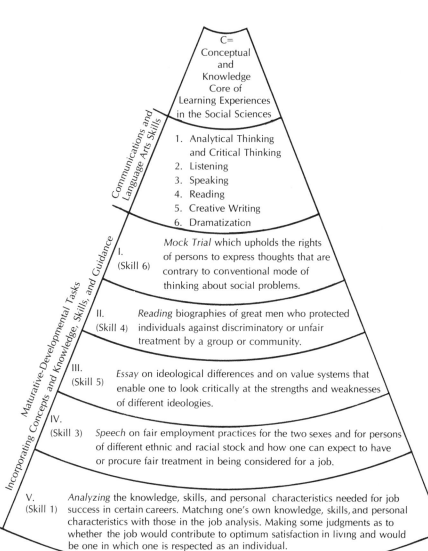

C=
Conceptual
and
Knowledge
Core of
Learning Experiences
in the Social Sciences

1. Analytical Thinking
   and Critical Thinking
2. Listening
3. Speaking
4. Reading
5. Creative Writing
6. Dramatization

I.
(Skill 6)   *Mock Trial* which upholds the rights
            of persons to express thoughts that are
            contrary to conventional mode of
            thinking about social problems.

II.
(Skill 4)   *Reading* biographies of great men who protected
            individuals against discriminatory or unfair
            treatment by a group or community.

III.
(Skill 5)   *Essay* on ideological differences and on value systems that
            enable one to look critically at the strengths and weaknesses
            of different ideologies.

IV.
(Skill 3)   *Speech* on fair employment practices for the two sexes and for persons
            of different ethnic and racial stock and how one can expect to have
            or procure fair treatment in being considered for a job.

V.
(Skill 1)   *Analyzing* the knowledge, skills, and personal characteristics needed for job
            success in certain careers. Matching one's own knowledge, skills, and personal
            characteristics with those in the job analysis. Making some judgments as to
            whether the job would contribute to optimum satisfaction in living and would
            be one in which one is respected as an individual.

NOTE: Arcs I-V represent experiences based on the following tasks described
in Havighurst's *Developmental Tasks and Education*.
I=Comprehending concepts and perfecting skills of citizenship. II=Assuming the
stance of and acting like a socially responsible adult. III=Formulating an in-
tegrative set of values and philosophy of life. IV=Becoming confident of one's
ability to become economically independent. V=Choosing a career which af-
fords optimum satisfaction in living.

Fig. 3 — Tri-Dimensional Model for Sequential and Integrated Learning in
English, Social Sciences, and Guidance, Illustrated by the Concept
of the Description and Protection of the Rights of Individuals

organizations, in assuming responsibility for persons and for products, and in appraising whether or not established goals have been met.

Steps in Sequencing Behavioral Objectives

In formulating a sequence of objectives, one should have in mind both a general goal and a more specific one. To achieve either goal, it becomes necessary to complete successfully a number of preparatory tasks. (Figure 4 illustrates this process

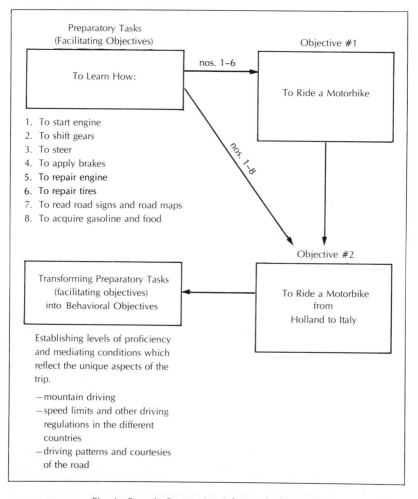

Fig. 4—Steps in Sequencing Behavioral Objectives

of specifying both the goals and the preparatory tasks. Each of the tasks in the example would require further delineation in the form of behavioral objectives.) Constructing sequences of objectives may be a discrete step-by-step approach, or it may be an approach that involves setting up a cumulative hierarchy in which skill or knowledge acquisition at one step becomes a part of each more complex succeeding step.

The following list summarizes the usual steps in sequencing behavioral objectives:

1. Determine what it is you want the learner to be able to do.
2. Define this objective in behavioral terms and identify mediating conditions, expected levels of proficiency, and methods for assessing proficiency.
3. Decide what are the preparatory tasks.
4. Cast the preparatory tasks into full-fledged behavioral objectives and order these along a continuum — or
5. Decide what the cumulative elements are in each of a number of objectives, and on this basis arrange the objectives in a taxonomic (hierarchical) structure. (See Figure 4.)

When sequencing certain types of objectives, one must, of course, be aware not only of the overlap of categories and sequences of objectives, but also of the cyclical and spiraling nature of the sequences. This is readily apparent in the growth of intellectual skills.

With a little practice, the reader can become skillful in preparing sequences that constitute a programed approach to achieving certain traits and abilities. For example, using the "Cognitive Domain" of the *Taxonomy*, this progression might be from knowledge acquisition to comprehension, and then on to application, analysis, synthesis, and evaluation. Using the "Affective Domain" of the *Taxonomy*, there might be a progression from receiving and responding to stimuli, to valuing and conceptualizing a value and organizing a value system, and then on to internalizing a set or predisposition to act on the basis of the value and value system.

By structuring a psychomotor domain, there would be a way of perceiving a third area of human development and a conceptual base for relating certain sequences of performance objectives. Optimum learning might involve programing a child through related and mutually reinforcing experiences in all three domains — cognitive, affective, and psychomotor.

Another model for sequencing can be illustrated by a simplified presentation of the need-objective continuum. Figures 5 and 6 suggest a flow of energy and activity from perceiving a need to formulating objectives and programs based upon this need. From there one might project and

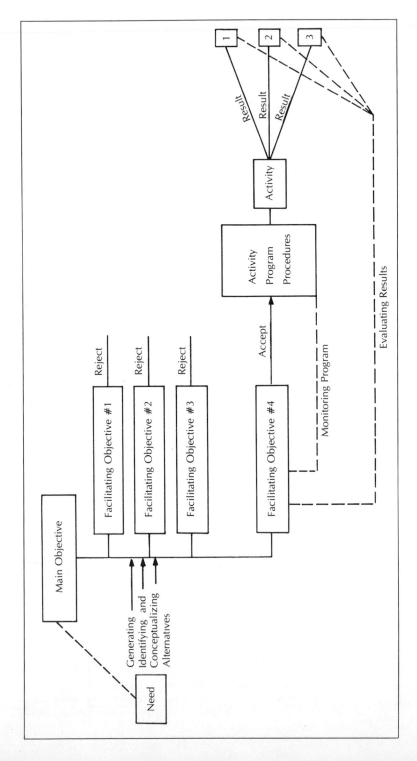

Fig. 5 — Need-Objective Continuum #1

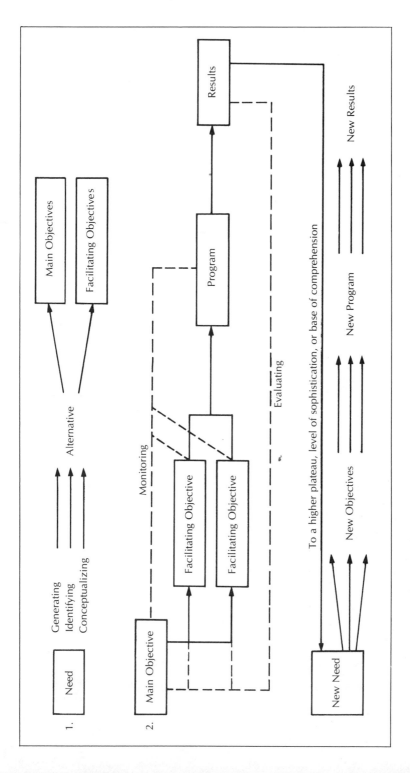

Fig. 6 — Need-Objective Continuum #2

1. Fact #1 → Fact #2 → Fact #3....

2. Fact → Concept

3. Concrete Experience → Abstract Representation of Experience

4. Skill #1 → Skill #2 → Skill #3....

5. Maturative or Developmental Level #1 → #2 → #3....
   Personal or Societal Developmental Task #1 → #2....[1]

6. Level of Awareness #1 → #2 → #3....
   6.1 Through sensitizing a person to his environment.
   6.2 Through sensitizing a person to relationships among persons, among institutions, and among data.
   6.3 Through multi-sensory experience.
   6.4 Through using and developing all the senses.

7. Level of Rationality #1 → #2 → #3....
   e.g. Comprehension and proposed solution to problem.
   7.1 Using additional facts, possibly from different subject-matter disciplines, to achieve successively higher levels of comprehension.
   7.2 Formulating more sophisticated definitions of the problem.
   7.3 Generating a number of possible solutions to the problems.

8. Ways of gathering data, solving problems, or of bringing about change
   8.1 Various strategies and processes, usually starting with gathering data and organizing it in some way and ending with either verification of solutions or institutionalization of an innovation.

9. Knowledge → Comprehension → Application → Analysis → Synthesis → Evaluation[2]

10. Cognition → Memory → Divergent Thinking → Evaluative Thinking[3]

Creative Process[4]
11. Preparation → Incubation → Illumination → Revision

Creative Skill
12. Awareness and sensitivity → Cognitive reordering of elements →
         to a situation   of the situation

    Search model formation → Verification of product and worth of product
         and testing

---

1. See reference Havighurst.
2. See reference Bloom et al.
3. See reference Guilford.
4. Graham Wallas, *The Art of Thought* (New York: Harcourt Brace & World, Inc., 1926). From E. Paul Torrance, *Guiding Creative Talent* (Englewood Cliffs, New Jersey: Prentice-Hall, Inc., 1962), p. 17.

Craftsmanship

13. Conceptualizing an → Preparing a plan → Selecting medium →
    object of art   and materials

    Choosing tools → Producing an object of art → Evaluating the product

Leadership

14. Getting other persons to engage in an activity or to carry out a task
    with few or no objections or interruptions.

    Planning → Motivating → Organizing → Coordinating →

    Protecting Followers → Evaluating

Fig. 7 — Types of Learning Sequences

evaluate results of activities and programs in light of the needs and objectives. Needless to say, the activity or program must be monitored in light of these same objectives.

A pertinent application of this need-objective continuum in education occurs when a teacher perceives a pupil's need and then proceeds to plan with him behavioral objectives and means by which he can achieve these objectives. The resulting learning activities can then be monitored and adjusted to facilitate optimum performance and the realization of objectives. Once an objective or group of objectives is achieved, the pupil may evidence a higher order of needs, which, in turn, calls for a higher order of main objectives.

Illustrative of an almost infinite array of learning sequences upon which we can pattern and program improvement in performance are those steps shown in Figure 7.

Examples of Sequences

Cognitive-Level Sequence

Before examining the first example of a sequence based on levels of cognition, we should remember that the cognitive level elicited by a given goal, question, or learning activity is related to the experiential background of the individual student. An item that elicits recall in one person may involve translation skills in another. For instance, when confronted with the word, *viviparous,* one student might respond, *"Viviparous* means . . ."* A second student might derive the meaning by translating the word from its Latin roots.

Illustrative of a cognitive-level sequence is the following sequence of behavioral objectives in biology. Each of the specific skills is identified in parentheses following the objective.

Step One. Working in groups of three, pupils construct an optimum environment of sunlight, nutrients, water, and heat for growing plants. They then plant three plants, a control group, in this environment. The groups of pupils can ask up to twenty questions, but after construction has started, they must complete this portion of the assignment without further help from the teacher. Environments constructed by each group are to be judged optimum on the basis of specified theories of plant growth. *(Knowledge, convergent thinking, and craftsmanship)*

Step Two. Each group of pupils is to vary environmental conditions of four sets of plants as follows:

1. Reduce exposure to sunlight one-half, but keep all other factors the same as in Step One.
2. Reduce nutrients one-half, but keep all other factors the same as in Step One.
3. Reduce water one-half, but keep all other factors the same as in Step One.
4. Reduce air temperature by 20°F., but keep all other factors the same as in Step One.

These conditions are to be created following a lecture and reading assignment on plant environments. Thus, we see the application of knowledge in creating experimental conditions. *(Application)*

Step Three. In their groups, the children are to observe at weekly intervals the growth of control, sunlight-deficient, nutrient-deficient, water-deficient, and heat-deficient groups of plants. They are to record in a notebook any observable changes in the growth of leaves, stems, and roots; in the formation of flowers and fruit; and in the leaf color. Then they are to determine how each of the four deficiencies affects the growth of various parts of the plants and the color of the leaves. Each group is to keep a notebook containing information showing how each experimental group of plants differs from the control group. *(Analysis)*

Step Four. Upon completing steps 1 through 3 to the satisfaction of the teacher, each group is to prepare a written report, including charts, diagrams, or time-lapse photographs, describing each of the steps and changes observed in control and experimental groups. A panel of three teachers representing the areas of biology, mathematics, and English should judge the group projects as "superior," using criteria discussed and agreed upon by the pupils for accuracy, resourcefulness, and originality. *(Synthesis)*

Step Five. Each group is to apply criteria for determining which of the following ingredients is most important and which is least important in plant growth: sunlight, water, nutrients, or heat. These criteria are the same ones that were developed by the teacher and the whole class prior to working on Step One. *(Evaluation)*

Review

An interesting way to practice the construction of cognitive-level sequences is to translate questions that have been framed according to the *Taxonomy* into statements of behavioral objectives. Translate each of the following questions into a behavioral objective without noting the cognitive level, and enter them on 3" × 5" cards. Then sequence your objectives without consulting the list of questions. If your final sequence is similar in order to the list of questions, you will have constructed a cognitive-level sequence. A different sequence is not necessarily wrong; it simply means that you may have changed the levels of the objectives in the translation. Your next task would be to determine how the level was changed.

1. What major formula of Albert Einstein paved the way to nuclear reactions? *(Knowledge)*
2. What does the formula $E=MC^2$ mean? *(Knowledge, comprehension-interpretation, or translation)*
3. Using your own words, describe each symbol in the above formula. *(Translation)*
4. How might our lives be different today if man had not discovered how to create atomic bombs and nuclear reactors used to generate electricity? *(Extrapolation)*
5. What relevance does $E=MC^2$ have for the construction of rocket engines and space vehicles? *(Application)*
6. Could the formula $E=MC^2$ be restated in terms of social energy, number of people in a group, and time required for social action, and then be used to interpret race riots, political campaigns, and advertising campaigns? *(Translation and application)*
7. What causative factors of revolutions are present in race, labor, and student riots in this country? *(Analysis)*
8. Recognizing major factors which contribute both to revolution and to cooperation, design a proposal by which persons throughout the world could live in eternal peace. *(Synthesis)*

9. Compare your proposal for eternal peace with Immanuel Kant's *Zum ewigen Frieden* (Perpetual Peace). *(Evaluation)*

10. Make a list of what you consider the five most important values undergirding our political-economic-social system. Which of these tend to be jeopardized by our participation in war? *(Evaluation)*[4]

Each of the behavioral objectives formulated should contain a clear statement of behavior, mediating conditions, and an expected level of proficiency. Crucial, of course, are behavioral meanings for each of the cognitive levels. If one or more elements are missing, it may be helpful to review Chapter 1 of this book and portions of Robert Mager's *Preparing Instructional Objectives* and discuss any problems with a co-worker.

Grade-Level Sequence

Illustrative of a grade-level sequence is the following list of social science behavioral objectives on health and safety.

Kindergarten. Children are to recognize and know how to respond to directions given by traffic-patrol boys and girls, traffic signals, and crosswalk markings. This is to be accomplished by having a traffic-patrol boy or girl demonstrate his duties in the classroom with a mock-up of traffic signals and crosswalk. Then a child will imitate the functions of the traffic patrol. The other children will obey his directions. This activity will be repeated several days until in the judgment of the teacher every child responds in a manner predetermined by the teacher as appropriate to the signals, crosswalk situation, and directions of the traffic-patrol child.

Grade One. After a unit on public services in the community, each of the pupils in the top reading group is to tell five things policemen do to protect citizens of the community.

Grade Two. As part of a culminating activity of a two-week study of the post office and telephone, each child in the class will write legibly and without error his phone number and address, including zip code.

Grade Four. To learn basic safety rules and the importance of cooperation, pupils serve as traffic-patrol officers. After each child has served one week on the traffic patrol, he should be

---

4. See Paul Plowman, "An Interpretation of the *Taxonomy of Educational Objectives*" (Sacramento: Paul Plowman, 1968), pp. 11–12.

able to tell his teacher three safety rules and three examples of how to maintain pedestrian safety through cooperation among patrol officers and other pupils.

Grade Five. In a study of the development of their state from frontier days to the present, pupils are to construct a mural portraying three ways law enforcement changed during that period.

Grade Eight. After studying services of the local, county, state, and federal government, students are to write 1000-word research papers on "Provisions for Inter-agency Cooperation in Times of Emergency." The papers should identify and describe three situations in which three or more of the agencies mentioned would work together in solving a problem or dealing with an emergency.

Grade Eleven. Following a series of units on the emergence of the United States as a world power, and in response to a quiz, each student is to give three examples of how the United States exercises policing powers outside its land area. Responses should include at least one of the following: patrol activity in our territorial waters; electronic monitoring of foreign military aircraft; and action singly or with other nations to stop aggression.

The preceding are objectives, for the most part, at the knowledge and comprehension levels of the *Taxonomy*. More significant and sophisticated lists would contain behavioral objectives that might be useful in developing traits in the "Affective Domain," higher cognitive skills, or creative skills.

Many of the behavioral objectives in this book have been graded to help the reader see the general level for which they are intended. In some instances one may disagree with the placement, recognizing that school experience, content acquisition, and skill development vary from state to state, from school to school, from class to class, and from pupil to pupil. A particular grade-level designation should not prevent the use of an objective in original or revised form at another grade level.

Review

To practice developing a graded sequence, select three graded objectives from this book or a curriculum guide, and rewrite them to make them appropriate for pupils two or more grade levels lower or higher than those stated. The use of cards is suggested.

Summary of Main Points

1. This chapter explores the rationale for preparing sequences of behavioral objectives. It identifies different types of progressions and suggests steps in framing sequences of behavioral objectives.

2. Sequences of behavioral objectives should be designed to be consistent with the needs of learners, the nature of the learning process, the requirements of effective teaching, and the nature of the content area.

3. Successful sequencing tends to create more rational group and individual learning activities.

4. One of the benefits to be derived from sequential behavioral objectives is the removal of the hit-and-miss nature of fragmented learning activities.

5. Behavioral objectives may be sequenced according to academic skills, maturative and developmental needs of individuals, or grade-level placement; development of creative, craftsmanship, and leadership skills; a need-objective continuum, or a combination of these in what might be called a learning-composite sequence.

Discussion Questions and Activities

The following questions and activities might profitably be utilized in group discussions.

1. What reasons can you give for sequencing behavioral objectives?

2. Upon what basis do you currently plan instructional-learning activities? Knowledge acquisition? Refinement of higher intellectual skills? Creative trait and skill development? Successful performance of developmental tasks?

3. What are the present strengths of your instructional program curriculum? Teaching guides? Lesson plans? How might they be bolstered further by applying some of the suggestions given in Chapters 1 and 2 of this book?

4. Starting with a given experience or set of data, what flexible sequences might result from idea generation, extrapolation, adaptative response, and divergent thought? Can we make provision for this type of activity in our classrooms?

5. Following a review of the qualities, characteristics, and functions of leaders, join with a small group of fellow teachers in developing a sequence of leadership objectives. These objectives should clearly describe the behavior sought, the levels of proficiency expected, and mediating conditions.

6. Formulate a personal or group plan of professional growth for developing skills and performance suggested in Chapters 1 and 2 of this book.

Bibliography

Ammerman, Harry L. "Some Important Ways in Which Performance Objectives Can Vary," *Deriving, Specifying, and Using Instructional Objectives*, by William H. Melching et al. Alexandria, Virginia: Human Resources Agency of George Washington University, 1966.

Anastasiow, Nicholas, and Jerman, Max. *An Introduction to Computer-Based Drill and Practice in Arithmetic.* New York: L. W. Singer, 1968.

Bloom, Benjamin, et al. *Taxonomy of Educational Objectives, Handbook I: Cognitive Domain.* New York: McKay, 1956.

Bruner, Jerome. *The Process of Education.* Cambridge: Harvard Univ. Press, 1966.

California State Department of Education. *Social Studies Framework for the Public Schools of California.* Sacramento: California State Department of Education, 1962.

Dave, R. H. "Taxonomy of Educational Objectives and Achievement Testing." Paper read at the International Conference on Educational Testing, May 1967, Berlin.

Featherstone, Joseph. "The Primary School Revolution in Britain," *The New Republic* 157, nos. 8–9 (1967).

Guilford, J. P. "Creativity: Its Measurement and Development," *A Source Book for Creative Thinking.* Edited by Sidney J. Parnes and Harold F. Harding. New York: Scribner's, 1962.

Hanna P. R., and Lee, J. R. *Generalizations from the Social Sciences,* 32d Yearbook, National Council of the Social Studies. Washington: National Education Association, 1962.

Havighurst, Robert J. *Developmental Tasks and Education.* New York: McKay, 1952.

Jourard, Sidney. "Healthy Personality and Self Disclosure," *Mental Hygiene* 43, no. 4 (October 1959): 499–507.

Krathwohl, David R.; Bloom, Benjamin; and Masia, B. B. *Taxonomy of Educational Objectives, Handbook II: Affective Domain.* New York: McKay, 1964.

Krug, Edward A. *Curriculum Planning.* New York: Harper & Brothers, 1950.

Los Angeles County Superintendent of Schools Office, Division of Elementary Education. *A Guide to Curriculum Development and Course of Study for Elementary Schools of Los Angeles County.* Los Angeles: Los Angeles County Superintendent of Schools Office, 1965.

Mager, Robert R. *Preparing Instructional Objectives.* Palo Alto, California: Fearon, 1962.

Maslow, Abraham H. *Toward a Psychology of Being.* New York: Van Nostrand, 1962.

May, Rollo. *Man's Search for Himself.* New York: Signet Books, 1967.

Plowman, Paul D. "An Interpretation of the Taxonomy of Educational Objectives." Sacramento, Calif.: Paul Plowman, 1968.

Torrance, E. Paul. *Guiding Creative Talent.* Englewood Cliffs, N.J.: Prentice-Hall, 1962.

Wallas, Graham. *The Art of Thought.* New York: Harcourt, Brace, 1926.

Whiston, Carole; Morton, Margaret; Bailey, Helen E. "The Oak Park Study Skills Chart," *The Instructor* 76 (April 1967): 63–74.

Winnetka Board of Education. *Supplement to the Social Studies Curriculum Guide.* Winnetka, Illinois: Winnetka Public Schools, 1967.

Yolo County Superintendent of Schools Office. *Social Studies Course of Study.* Woodland, Calif.: Yolo County Superintendent of Schools Office, 1964.

CHAPTER 3

ENGLISH AND LITERATURE

3

Why English and Literature Are Taught

How English and Literature Are Taught

Gauging Pupil Growth and Effectiveness

Academic Skills

Creative and Higher Cognitive Skills

Persons who teach English and literature have an awesome responsibility, for within these curricula are transmitted communication skills, value patterns, and student self-concepts. How does a teacher of English and literature guide student performance in a positive direction? How do his activities leave a catalytic residue that affects the scholastic direction of his students during their school years and throughout their adult lives? This chapter attempts to provide answers to these questions, which can lead to improved competence and satisfaction in teaching.

Why English and Literature Are Taught

One main purpose in teaching English is to improve students' thinking and communications skills. Educators are concerned about aspects of comprehension—the ability of a pupil to interpret the printed page and the spoken word; to translate the symbols he sees into meaningful thoughts; to solve problems through analyzing and evaluating the technique and content of a written or spoken work as well as the motives of the creator; and to synthesize in words the essence of human experience and aspiration.

In studying literature, children come in contact with human experience; they consider ideas and vicariously become a part of another person's thoughts and experiences. Through literature we give children the opportunity to feel, to value, to experience, to appreciate, and possibly to create. In becoming acquainted with literature, pupils compare thoughts of eminent writers and grapple with the great ideas of mankind. They can make some judgments about styles of thinking, communicating, persuading, and expressing thoughts, and possibly achieve personal commitment to them. From literature children acquire models of written expression and a greater understanding of the history and projected future of man. They are exposed to different value systems and, of great importance, they learn to laugh and to experience joy in encounters with their fellow man.

How English and Literature Are Taught

Words are obviously building blocks of oral and written communication. The effective use of words and of patterns of words is characterized by efficiency and artistry in listening, speaking, reading and writing.

Words and themes, the fundamental elements of literature, are arranged into structures such as phrases, sentences, paragraphs, short stories, novels, plays, poems, speeches, and essays. An analysis of the structure includes an appraisal of style, format and grammar.

Language Skills

Listening, speaking, reading, writing, and spelling are skills of language. They occupy a major portion of the primary teacher's time and are also stressed in the middle grades. Each subject area at every grade level demands continual reinforcement of these skills: care in listening, precision in speaking and writing, accuracy in spelling, and reading analysis, speed, and comprehension. Teachers in every area may help students comprehend and become facile in the use of verbal symbols. This implies more than just being able to spell and to use the right word at the right time. It also implies housing these symbols within the context of grammatical structure and accepted usage, and developing flexibility, fluency, and originality in expressing thoughts.

Although these skills tend to be taught in isolation, they are learned most effectively in a unified approach to developing the individual. This may mean developing language skills within, or at least relating them to, the broader explorations of literature, communication, clear thinking, and acquisition of values. The emphasis should be upon life and meaning and upon the use and generative aspects of elements, rather than upon identification or critical analysis of the parts of speech or elements of a sentence alone.

Literature Skills

The skills of literature are primarily those of analysis, assessment, and appreciation. They are related to and interwoven within the context of higher cognitive, affective, and creative skill development. They involve and reinforce the language skills of critical listening, reading, creative writing, and spelling. The skills of literature are also directed toward helping children do the following:

1. Understand the literary heritages and cultures of English-speaking countries and other countries
2. Appreciate cultural conflicts and the interplay of political forces in history
3. Experience vicariously great historical events, contact with eminent persons, and moments of great joy and sadness
4. Develop discrimination and taste
5. Gain a broad base of experience for self-understanding and personal development
6. Raise their own levels of aspiration
7. View their own problems of development in the light of similar problems that have been resolved by fictitious as well as by real people
8. Acquire values that tend to direct and integrate subsequent experience
9. Develop a philosophy of life

Terms such as *understand, appreciate,* and *experience* have been used in the preceding list; these are general, non-behavioral goals for English and literature. Perhaps the behavioral aspects of a literature program are better illustrated by the following:

1. Recalling key facts and episodes
2. Involving oneself vicariously in the experiences of characters in a story, novel, or poem
3. Ferreting out an author's meaning
4. Going beyond the printed word in drawing inferences
5. Relating literature to past and present social, political, and economic problems and events
6. Using prose and poetry as media for examining and internalizing values.
7. Gaining from literature the models of style and the techniques for creating effects which can be applied in one's own oral and written communication

The elements, structures, principles, and skills of English tend to be taught in isolation. There may be some justification for such a concentrated emphasis. However, another point of view is that literature and language are woven inextricably into all learning experiences: words, paragraphs, rules of grammar, and the skills of listening, speaking, reading, and writing may reinforce and enhance each other through classroom experience.

In teaching English, the teacher emphasizes mastery of vocabulary and the use and interpretation of words while listening, speaking, reading, and writing. This means that the teacher must assess the current levels of a child's comprehension and communication skills, and prescribe activities and experiences that will result in a measurable or observable level of improved performance. To help in this assessment, there is promising work being done to develop and apply techniques of diagnosis and prescription in the experimental materials and field testing of *Individually Prescribed Instruction,* by Research for Better Schools, Inc. of Philadelphia, Pennsylvania. *Individually Prescribed Instruction,* the SRA *Reading Laboratory®* series, and other published skill-development programs occupy a position somewhere between that of kits of progressive skill-improvement assignments, developed by individual teachers, and computer-assisted instruction.

Gauging Pupil Growth and Effectiveness

There are a number of routes that might be taken in appraising the effectiveness of a language or literature program. One of these would be to determine what facts children know upon completion of an English program that they did not know before becoming involved in it. Broadly standardized or teacher-made achievement tests are often used to compare the effectiveness of educational programs in a state, school district, or individual school.

Another means of gauging pupil growth and effectiveness of a program is to note any changes in pupil attitudes, interests, and feelings. Teachers might ask themselves, "To what extent are these children more sensitive, more flexible, more tolerant, and more humane? To what extent are they more open and more creative?" This area deals with the affective domain, and is fraught with the many pitfalls inherent in the making of subjective judgments. Yet it is possible to observe and rate these characteristics.

Sometimes all that teachers have to do is to observe the number and the kinds of books a child reads, the topics he chooses for written and oral assignments, and his use of unstructured time. This leads to another means of assessment, which is to examine the products: the themes, speeches, poems, plays, essays, and short stories a pupil produces, as well as the results of grammar and spelling tests.

Sociograms and other observation checklists can be used to note the effect that improved language skills have upon:

1. A child's increased acceptance by his peers and by his teachers
2. His participation in activities which require some ability in speaking and writing
3. His recognition of his own leadership ability and his worth as a person

It is also important to ascertain the extent to which the child has developed skills of thinking and of expressing himself. There may be growth in higher cognitive skills, such as the ability to analyze an event, a process, a structure, or a product; the ability to create a beautiful poem or a moving story; or the ability to apply a set of criteria or standards in determining the merit of a literary product. Evaluative criteria are clearly outlined in textbooks and numerous curriculum guides for such skills of English as writing, spelling, listening, speaking, and reading.

Review

Before proceeding, you may find it helpful to test your understanding of the concepts advanced in Chapter 1, and of their application in the subject areas of English and literature, by answering the following questions:

1. What is a behavioral objective?
2. What are four distinguishing features of this type of objective?
3. Which of the following are behavioral objectives that contain clear descriptions of observable or measurable behavior, as well as levels of proficiency for that behavior?
   a. The student is to describe a humorous event in such a way that he elicits spontaneous laughter from members of the class.
   b. Students are to make literature live.
   c. After three weeks of instruction and practice, the student is to debate the issue, "Resolved: All eighteen-year-old persons should be allowed to vote in national and state elections."
   d. After witnessing a dramatic reenactment of the Gettysburg Address, the student, within a five-minute period, is able to list three key ideas expressed by President Lincoln. Satisfactory completion of this assignment is to be judged by the comparison of responses with the content of the speech in a history book, by the teacher timing the student, and by the application of teacher-student agreed-upon criteria as to what constitutes a key idea.

Objectives 3*a* and 3*d* use words that denote observable or measurable behavior and levels of proficiency. To prove to yourself that you recognize these elements of behavioral objectives, complete the questions below:

4. What words denote observable or measurable behavior in 3*a*? In 3*d*?
5. List the levels of proficiency specified in 3*a* and in 3*d*.

Now compare notes with other persons reading this book. Are your responses similar or different? If different, why? Is there room for some difference in interpretation?

When you scrutinized objectives 3*a* and 3*d*, did you notice words denoting *conditions* under which the behavior was to be performed or *methods* for determining whether or not proficiency levels had been reached? Identify conditions and methods in objectives 3*a* and 3*d*. Again, if possible, compare your answers with a co-worker. To compare your responses with designations by the author, turn to page 60.

At this point, you may want to review portions of Chapter 1. Also helpful might be a review of relevant sections of two books: Mager's *Preparing Instructional Objectives,* and Popham's *The Teacher Empiricist—A Curriculum and Study Supplement.*

6. Determine which of the four elements of behavioral objectives (description of behavior, mediating conditions, proficiency levels, and methods of measuring) are included in, and which are missing from, objectives 3*b* and 3*c*.
7. Rewrite objectives 3*b* and 3*c*, making the descriptions of behavior and the performance levels clear and succinct. Be sure to spell out the conditions and indicate methods by which the performance level will be evaluated.

After this review and practice, behavioral objectives stressing academic skills, higher cognitive skills, and creative skills will be considered separately. The categories of behavioral objectives overlap quite naturally at certain points. This is particularly evident in the intimate relationship of certain traits of creativity and certain higher cognitive skills. Certainly efforts to extend human awareness, sensitivity, flexibility, and fluency in thought, and the ability to toy with a whole range of ideas have a very direct impact on man's rationality and functioning intelligence. An indication of rationality and intelligence is one's ability to consider facts from a number of areas in solving problems and to consider all possible alternatives, or at least an optimum number, in making a decision or solving a problem. Productive divergent thinking is, indeed, an earmark of human intelligence.

Academic Skills

Listening

A child listens for a host of reasons. He searches for clues from his social and natural environment as to how to act and react. Listening is a means of obtaining information and a means of enjoyment, both of which can be improved through careful attention to various parts of what he hears. For example, when he is listening to a sound composition, a child should ascertain similarities and differences within the composition and compare the composition to others. He should listen for themes, for main ideas, and for words, tones, and rhythms that create certain effects. He should also listen so that he might appreciate and enjoy sounds and combinations, and derive meaning from the sounds he hears. Examples of behavioral objectives in listening are:

1. By the end of the first grade, eighty percent of the pupils will be able to discriminate similarities and differences in sounds in simple words such as *hat, mat, bat, pat, rat, rot, full, fill,* etc. The teacher is to determine which children are to be guided by this objective and is to assess this behavior through talking with each pupil.

2. Following instruction and practice in detecting sequences of ideas and facts in various speeches, students listen to a three-minute speech and, with no more than one error, place in proper sequence five facts or ideas presented.

3. Upon hearing a poem, high-school students tell three words or series of words used to create the mood of the poem.

4. After hearing a recording of a mystery story, fifth-grade students recall, with no more than two errors, five words used to create a mood of mystery.

5. To demonstrate an understanding of the teacher's spoken directions, students proceed in correct sequence in (a) doing an assignment, or (b) playing a game.

6. Following instruction in the principles of speech construction and delivery, eleventh-grade students listen to speeches by a minister, a governor, the president of the United States, or a United Nations delegate and then prepare lists of speech construction and delivery principles followed and violated in the presentations. This is to be done by filling out a listening checklist prepared in advance by the students and teacher.

7. As a homework assignment, pupils are to list all the different sounds they hear during a twenty-minute period at night. The list should contain at least ten different sounds.

Speaking

A person's speech is a mirror reflecting his experiences, his culture, his emotions, his logic, and his training. Speech may be highly controlled or casual. It may pave the way to social and business success, or it may brand a person as vulgar or undesirable and shut the door to certain types of employment.

Through speaking, a student is able to express his ideas and his individuality. By providing opportunities for success in speaking, the teacher may foster self-confidence, personal development, maturity, and the ability to present ideas and convince others. Improvement in the skills of speech results from careful study of a student's previous experiences, his maturity, and his need to express himself. Speaking is a learned skill; it is a skill that is improved through practice and careful guidance. Examples of behavioral objectives in speaking are:

1. In a "show-and-tell" period, pupils demonstrate their ability to convey information accurately. Each pupil is to report to the class at least three characteristics of an unusual object he has brought from home.
2. Seventh-grade students demonstrate the use of visual aids, such as maps, charts, and overlay transparencies, to augment five-minute speeches on contemporary affairs which they present to the class. These demonstrations are to be judged satisfactory by a student panel which applies agreed-upon criteria.
3. After studying and practicing speech techniques for creating effects, twelfth-grade students present four-minute speeches designed to influence class opinion on (a) certain steps taken by students to solve their own problems, or (b) certain programs advocated by politicians to solve problems of unemployment, hunger, or unsanitary living conditions. The extent of success in influencing the class will be assessed by a questionnaire determining whether each member of the class was "completely convinced," "convinced but with some reservations," or "not convinced."
4. By the time a child is in third grade, he should be able to give the correct sounds for the diagraphs *th, ch, sh,* and *ph.*
5. By the end of the second grade, the child should be able to distinguish between pairs of voiced and voiceless consonants, such as *b-p, c-g,* and *f-y.*

Reading

Reading is still the center of the school experience and the acculturation of the child. Although sound and picture and sound devices (such as tape recorders, television, and computer-assisted instruction) are gaining popularity as teaching tools, teachers are quick to assert the importance of the printed word and of the textbook. This situation may change in time, but for the present, the educational process is largely dependent upon the printed word.

Through reading, a child enters a world of fantasy in which he vicariously assumes innumerable roles and reacts to innumerable situations. He may experience through his reading a wide range of human emotions. Hopefully his reading will lead to inspiration and higher aspirations. As a result of school-required, job-related, and avocational reading, a child becomes a different person—more knowledgeable, insightful, creative, and humane. Examples of behavioral objectives in reading are:

1. Primary-grade pupils in the top reading group are to demonstrate correct spatial orientation by distinguishing between the letters *u* and *n, p* and *q, d* and *b,* and *m* and *w* by the time they reach the third grade. They demonstrate this ability by reading, with no more than five errors per one hundred words, appropriate selections from their basic readers. Assessment is to be done by the teacher.

2. After instruction and practice in the use of the SRA *Reading Laboratory®* series, pupils judged by the teacher as capable of independent work are to read and test their own progress through the whole series of reading and power-builder cards in a given laboratory without further direction from the teacher.

3. Students in the top reading group are to research the topic "Preservation of Birds" in three different encyclopedias. They are then to indicate (a) which encyclopedia presents the idea or topic most clearly, (b) which provides the most information, and (c) which best augments the text through pictures, diagrams, and charts. Responses will be compared with professional educators' reviews of the same encyclopedias. There should be sixty percent agreement among students' and educators' responses.

4. After a study of the most common prefixes, eighth-grade students are to define with no more than one error each of the following prefixes and to write two words containing each prefix: *ad-, be-, dis-, pre-, re-,* and *sub-*.

5. After a study of the techniques of skimming and scanning, and after practicing two eye fixations per line of printed matter, recalling main ideas and details, and using a tachistoscope, students in tenth-grade college-preparatory English are to test their reading speed and comprehension. The tests should show an increase of 200 percent in students' effective reading rates (number of words per minute

multiplied by the percent of comprehension questions answered correctly).

Writing

When man discovered that he could record his thoughts, his experiences, his commands, his inventory of possessions, his trade and business transactions, and his laws on tablets of stone, on canvas, or on paper, he became able to extend his power and his influence. His written communications went where he could not go, recording and fostering a rule of law among men and helping business enterprises to grow and flourish.

Unfortunately, writing skills are often neglected or pursued with a minimum of diligence by both teacher and pupil. Of the language skills, writing remains the one most often neglected or inadequately taught. Examples of behavioral objectives in writing are:

1. After a trip to the zoo, first-grade pupils are to use their picture dictionaries and copy the names of at least six animals they saw.
2. Sixth-grade pupils prepare simple outlines on topics of special interest to them, and write articles for a bulletin board newspaper or a children's literary magazine describing their interests. No more than five errors of grammar should be made for every 200 words.
3. After receiving instruction on various forms of writing, students are to write (a) a sonnet on human joy, (b) an essay on social problems in America, (c) a set of directions, (d) a book or movie review, or (e) a narrative account of a personal experience.
4. Following a week of practice in using transitional words, students in journalism class are to use in their own writing sixty percent of the transitional words on a teacher-prepared list.

Related Academic Skills

Other skills that are related to the study of English and literature include recalling facts and episodes, putting oneself into the context of experience portrayed by the author, and discerning the author's meaning and his intent. Equally important literature skills are: relating literature to the many dimensions of human experience—historical, social, political, economic, esthetic, and religious; using literature as a means of examining, vicariously testing, and acquiring values; and gaining from literature understandings and techniques for improving the impact of one's own verbal and written communication.

Recalling Facts and Episodes. This skill requires the child to maintain an attentive set. An example of a behavioral objective in this area is:

> After listening to the teacher read a story, the child is to tell the class the main elements of the story. The teacher and a majority of the class members should verify the child's responses.

Vicariously Testing and Acquiring Values. Through putting himself into the context created by an author, a child can try out different roles and values. A behavioral objective in this skill area is:

> After reading an adventure story, sixth-grade students describe how they felt as they read about a conflict in the story. This description should, in the opinion of the teacher, show that the student was vicariously testing his own values.

Discerning the Author's Meaning. To interpret the meaning of statements and situations encountered in his reading, a child draws upon his own background of experience. One behavioral objective promoting this skill is:

> Twelfth-grade students in a college-preparatory class are to read one of Shakespeare's plays. Each member of the class is to explain the meaning of a passage selected by the teacher. This interpretation is to be verified by citing one or more recognized Shakespearean scholars.

Relating Literature to Life. Without indulging in preciosity, it can be said that literature is a reflection and a portrayal of life, of man in all his moods and circumstances. And there is an essence of literature that abides within the educated man and carries him through the rough spots of life. A behavioral objective that helps relate literature to flesh and blood, to despair and joy, to greed and compassion, or to life and death of the spirit might be:

> After reading a play or story, junior-high students demonstrate their understanding and interpretation by producing and performing a version of the play or story.

Improving Verbal and Written Communication. Writing is a disciplined task, calling for attention to accuracy, style, intended audience, and desired effect. Like the speaker, the writer may direct his efforts toward informing, entertaining, motivating, and convincing others. One way to become sophisticated in performing these functions is to read model compositions. Analysis is needed to discern the style and techniques of each artist, but once techniques are recognized they can be emulated. In selecting models, we should consider contemporary writers who have had great impact upon their readers, as well as famous classical writers. A behavioral objective stated as an assignment might be:

> Learn the techniques used by four modern American writers to inform, entertain, motivate, and convince. Then, (1) find an example of how each of the following persons used one or more of these techniques in their writing: Aristophanes, Shakespeare, Samuel Adams, Edgar Allan Poe, and Winston Churchill; and (2) apply four or more of the techniques used by the authors studied in writing a speech, an essay, a short story, and a poem.

Creative and Higher Cognitive Skills

English and literature are natural domains of creative activity — whether one is thinking of Shakespeare, Shelley, and Sandburg, or of the creative listening, speaking, acting and writing activities of a fifth-grade student.

There are ample opportunities in English and literature programs for cultivating a creative attitude and for helping pupils apply the creative process. In listening and reading, a pupil can extend awareness of other peoples, other environments, other thoughts, and other resources, and overcome the obstacles of space and time. Through speaking, and through the reactions of other persons to what he has to say, a pupil can get an idea of his own effectiveness and become more self-aware. In writing, a pupil has the opportunity to produce original and worthwhile products.

What teachers should strive for is improvement in the quality of educational experiences and in the quality of human beings. When children under our tutelage become more creative, compassionate, and humane, and when they become more skillful in the use of their intellects, we indeed merit the appellation *teacher.* To accomplish this goal, however, we

have to enter into transactional, affective, dialogical relationships with children. We and they have to be honest with one
another as persons—and not behave solely as teachers and
pupils.[1] This thought suggests that we see pupils in the full
range of their being, so that we can develop them fully for their
benefit and for the ultimate benefit of our society and way of
life.

Some people would say that what we seek is *enrichment,*
an improvement in the quality of educational experience in
ways that deliberately improve the perceptual, intellectual,
and creative traits of the children with whom we are working.
This definition must be made more functional, must be translated into behavioral terms, if it is to be useful to the teacher.

What is meant by "improvement in the quality of educational experience"? What are the "ways" to use in the process
of improvement? To what extent are the traits observable and
measurable? Hopefully, answers to these questions will become evident as we progress through this book and as the
quality of educational experience in our classrooms reflects
concern for deliberate development of higher cognitive and
creative traits of individuals.

The field of literature abounds with opportunities for sens-
ing, elaborating, and appreciating, through analyzing and
synthesizing past knowledge, understandings, and feelings.
We bring ourselves to the printed page and come away in
some measure changed by what we have read.

The teacher of literature can design a myriad of questions
and assignments to foster recall of facts and episodes. The
skill of discerning an author's meaning requires a much more
advanced cognitive skill, analysis. Comprehension and its
subskills—interpretation, translation, and extrapolation—
should be woven into the fabric of good literature programs.
Application of standards of taste and coverage is another
skill to be developed in such programs.

As indicated previously, a teacher's problem is often one of
emphasis. He must determine how much time to spend at each
of the various cognitive levels. A good technique for a teacher
to use is to turn on a tape recorder for a class period. Then, in
the safety of his workroom or living room, or together with
other teachers, he can find out what amount of time and what
percentage of his questions are involved merely with the
absorption and retrieval of facts. A teacher should not be surprised to find he spends eighty to ninety-five percent of his
time at this lowest of all cognitive levels. Most teachers do
just that.

1. See Gardner Murphy, *Freeing Intelligence Through Teaching* (New York:
Harper & Row, 1961).

There is a professional rebirth going on, and a part of this has to do with teachers becoming orchestrators of higher intellectual skills and specific traits of creativity. But teachers don't become orchestrators overnight. What teachers can do is to start preparing behavioral objectives to help them become facile in creating experiences and opportunities which, besides providing basic concepts and facts, also help children awaken to the world and reach out and touch it with a host of perceptual, intellectual, and creative skills.

Examples of Behavioral Objectives

The following behavioral objectives are examples of those that advance higher cognitive and creative skills. In parentheses after each objective is an indication of the skill developed or the cognitive level.

1. To develop fluency in expression, students are to write sentences containing the following ideas:
   (a) All persons are important: children and adults; educated and uneducated persons; businessmen and unskilled laborers; and persons of all races.
   (b) True patriots are those who demonstrate their love for their country not only through words but also through actions.
   (c) One of a person's most valuable possessions is friendship.
   Each member of the class should write three sentences which, in the judgment of a committee of three students, convey the same ideas. *(Fluency)*
2. Students are to listen to and read reports concerning the causes of violence and ways of combating the spread of violent behavior and crimes against persons. Each student is to prepare an original statement in news-release format and style. The statement should propose five principles the mayor or city manager of a community might follow in making a city safer for children, young adults, middle-aged persons, and old people. Persons familiar with the sources used by the students should form a panel to identify the elements in each student's written synthesis. *(Application and synthesis)*
3. Students are to prepare and present to their class five-minute informal talks on pressure groups. In the opinion of a person with a college major in political science, the talks should provide convincing, sufficiently comprehensive, and valid answers to the following questions: (a) Are pressure groups necessary? (b) Do they reduce or augment a person's political power? (c) What abuses of pressure groups endanger freedom and security? *(Synthesis)*

4. After reading a story concerning how a young person's values were tested by classmates or neighbors and strengthened by the testing, the student is to prepare a presentation with tape recorder, colored slides, and overlays to show how reading certain books may contribute to the development of one's values. This presentation is to be observed by an English teacher, an audio-visual specialist, a cinematographer, or an author of children's stories. *(Synthesis and interpretation)*

5. Students are to listen to speeches by three political candidates, and analyze and evaluate each speech as to whether or not (a) the candidates presented basically different and conflicting points of view; (b) there were any clues as to the sincerity or lack of sincerity of the candidates; (c) what was said enabled listeners to decide which candidate would be best for the office; and (d) what was said might appreciably affect, positively or negatively, the chances of each candidate to win the election. In the opinion of the teacher, analyses should identify data which could be used in answering the questions, and evaluations should involve formulation and application of valid criteria. *(Analysis and evaluation)*

Discussion Questions and Activities

If possible, arrange to discuss the following questions and do the practice exercises in small groups.

1. Why do we teach English?

2. Why do we teach literature?

3. What higher cognitive and creative skills might be developed in an English program?

4. What steps would you take to develop higher cognitive and creative skills in or through listening, speaking, reading, and writing?

5. What higher cognitive and creative skills might be developed in a literature program?

6. Prepare one behavioral objective for improving (a) a skill of listening, (b) a skill of speaking, (c) a skill of reading, and (d) a skill of writing. Discuss these objectives with co-workers. Be sure that your objectives contain a clear description of behavior, established levels of proficiency, methods to determine if they have been reached, and a description of conditions under which the performance or behavior will be observed or tested.

7. Prepare one behavioral objective for each of the skills of literature listed on page 46.

8. Prepare a behavioral objective in English for each of the English skills and for each of the five categories of behavioral objectives. If possible, have a co-worker review your statements to be sure that each contains the four distinguishing features of behavioral objectives.

Answers to Review Questions

Pages 48–49:

Elements Present		Elements Missing
3b		B, C, P, and M
3c	B, C	P and M

Pages 48–49: Analysis of behavioral objectives 3a and 3d.

3a Behavior: To describe
   Level(s) of Proficiency: To elicit spontaneous laughter
   Conditions: Presentation to the class
   Method of Assessing
      Proficiency: Not given
   (optional)

Note: In this objective, the behavior might have been further delineated with words denoting an oral description. The method of assessment, although not stated, might simply be hearing the laughter.

3d Behavior: To list
   Level(s) of Proficiency: (1) Within a five-minute
                                   period
                               (2) "Key" ideas that
                                   meet agreed-upon
                                   criteria
                               (3) Ideas that match
                                   the content of the
                                   Gettysburg Address
   Conditions: Having listened to and
                                   observed a dramatic pre-
                                   sentation
   Method: (1) Timing
                               (2) Matching
                               (3) Applying criteria

Bibliography

California State Department of Education. *English Language Framework for California Public Schools, K–12.* Sacramento: California State Department of Education, 1968.

Carlson, Ruth Kearney. *Sparkling Words.* Champaign, Ill.: National Council of Teachers of English, 1965.

Grose, Lois M.; Miller, Dorothy; and Stein, Erwin R. *Suggestions for Evaluating Junior High School Writing.* Champaign, Ill.: National Council of Teachers of English, 1963.

Jenkinson, Edward B., and Hawley, Jane Stauder, eds. *Teaching Literature in Grades Seven Through Nine.* Champaign, Ill.: National Council of Teachers of English, 1967.

Leavitt, Hart Day, and Sohn, David A. *Stop, Look, and Write!* New York: Bantam Books, 1964.

Moffett, James. *Drama: What Is Happening.* Champaign, Ill.: National Council of Teachers of English, 1967.

Murphy, Gardner. *Freeing Intelligence Through Teaching,* 2d ed. New York: Harper & Row, 1961.

Pettit, Dorothy. *Poetry in the Classroom.* Champaign, Ill.: National Council of Teachers of English, 1966.

CHAPTER 4

SOCIAL SCIENCE

4

What Is Taught in Social Science

How Social Science Is Taught

A Holistic Approach to the Study of Man

Academic Skills

Higher Cognitive Skills

Creative Skills

Leadership Skills

Who is man? What has he achieved? What might he become? Attempts to answer such questions are found in the research studies and speculative writings of philosophers and poets, anthropologists and historians, sociologists and psychologists, economists and political scientists, and geographers and archeologists. These thinkers, most of them social scientists, represent organized areas of knowledge, structures of data, concepts, generalizations, and principles that help us comprehend and interpret the nature of man, the social animal. But still needed is a holistic view of man, not as an instrument of material progress or of governmental authority, not as a dehumanized performer of societal roles, but as an entity.

This chapter deals with developing behavioral objectives in the social sciences. Topics such as the community, American history, American government, and economics are covered. Also treated is a multidisciplinary approach to the study of these areas which is valuable in analyzing and comprehending the social dynamic in which man extends and defines himself.

What Is Taught in Social Science

In his encounter with the social sciences, the pupil will be involved in interpreting, inferring, and classifying knowledge, both in his own unique ways and in accordance with established criteria or certain models of investigation. He may also be engaged in observing, measuring, and describing social phenomena.

Community Studies

Man is a part of a matrix of interweaving social spheres and a number of increasingly broader communities—local, state, regional, and international. Each community is formed of a group of interacting persons, unified by common geographical, cultural, economic, or social conditions and interests. Members of the community perform tasks for its perpetuation, and seek from it certain services and opportunities.

In the past, community studies tended to analyze and describe roles performed by individual members of the community, such as community service-workers and leaders, as well as the roles of various groups within the community, and of governmental and civic organizations. In addition, the goals and methods of business and industry, schools, other governmental agencies, and public utilities were studied.

Today it is generally agreed that the study of man in his communities should be concerned with more than man's role as a societal agent. Concern should instead be with the dynamics of community development, management, perpetuation, and change. The curriculum should also highlight the impact of community and environment upon the individual in relation to his personal, social, political, legal, and economic affairs, and focus as well upon how man relates to and changes his community. Today's community studies are increasingly concerned with environmental problems and the preservation of individual rights.

Skills in community studies include:

1. Acquiring knowledge basic to civic competence
2. Comprehending and interpreting community goals, problems, and events
3. Participating in local civic affairs
4. Learning how to effect change in governmental policies, economic conditions, political actions, and social relationships
5. Communicating effectively with persons and organizations in a community
6. Applying principles of group dynamics, social psychology, and persuasion
7. Providing leadership

American History

History is the story of significant change in man and his environment. It is studied to understand the meaning of events and the causative forces, geography, cultural developments, and social relations involved in those events. It is studied to understand the dynamics of leadership in the lives of men who have fashioned or influenced social, economic, and political institutions and events. History is a matter of perspective, perception, and subjective decisions about what events are significant to man and his environment.

History is studied in order to understand the dynamics of change in man and his environment. From history we can gain an understanding of why an idea or event was labeled significant by persons who lived in the past, or by contemporary historians who interpret the past in light of current events and project the continuum of man's experience and his culture into the future. We study history to place ourselves within the mainstream of historical events and of the record of mankind—his progress and his lack of it; his creative power and his spent energy; his grand achievements and his ignominious defeats; his nobility and his baseness; his excellence and his mediocrity.

Some of the basic skills of American history are:

1. Acquiring knowledge of significant changes in man and his environment
2. Interpreting and analyzing an event from a number of perspectives
3. Applying different criteria in judging the significance of events
4. Ferreting out the causes of particular events
5. Assessing the reasons for diplomatic and military successes and failures
6. Gaining skill in reflective and analytical thinking
7. Synthesizing one's understanding of patriotism and one's feelings of pride, doubt, or dissatisfaction with steps that America took in becoming a nation and a leader in international affairs
8. Judging the relevance of historical studies to an understanding of America today
9. Recognizing important steps in the development of our democratic society and way of life
10. Developing techniques for gathering, organizing, and interpreting facts about historical events, periods, problems, and accomplishments
11. Knowing where to locate historical facts and authoritative interpretations of historical events
12. Knowing how to verify a fact and how to apply scientific methods to the study of American history

American Government

The study of American government involves the elements, structures, and functions of political authority and power. In a dynamic sense it investigates the making of decisions and the establishment of policies and values. The study of government is concerned with human behavior, and with the activities of institutions that exert power or that affect the general welfare. In studying American government, the student learns steps that have been taken and must still be taken to fashion "a more perfect union" out of the diverse elements of community, state, and nation.

Two concepts underlying the American governmental system are *authority* and *responsibility*. It is commonly recognized that administrative authority rests in certain prerogatives. Key among these are the formulation of policy, the direction and administration of men and organizations, and the utilization of monetary resources. But in a very real sense there is little authority unless there is acquiescence.[1] And there is little general acquiescence to involvement in governmental programs unless there is leadership based upon the "authority of knowledge,"[2] respect for skill in governing programs and personnel, and application of sound operating principles. If authority rests upon acquiescence and respect, governmental leaders must look inwardly at themselves as well as outwardly at the parameters and variables of their jobs. The word *responsibility* implies that leaders respond affectively and effectively to perceived needs and to the requirements of their designated and perceived roles as administrators.

Skills of American government include the following:

1. Understanding the system of American government
2. Applying economic, political, and social theory in analyzing and interpreting the purposes, structures, and functions of American government
3. Comprehending·the rights of American citizens
4. Judging the effectiveness of the American political system
5. Applying principles of American government to class and school activities

Economics

The study of economics is the study of man engaged in the production, consumption, and use of goods and services. It is the study of the allocation of human and material resources and of the way man organizes his energies to supply his basic needs. It is the study of the creation and gratification of material wants, and of supply and demand, trading and competition, and creation and deployment of capital.

1. See Chester Barnard, *Functions of the Executive*, 2nd ed. (Cambridge, Massachusetts: Harvard University Press, 1968).
2. See J. B. Sears, *The Nature of the Administrative Process* (New York: McGraw-Hill, 1950), pp. 231–32.

Economics can be an intensely interesting and important part of the curriculum, an area of study affecting the lives of all persons. In the past it was often avoided because it was taught in a highly abstract and esoteric manner, but today economics can be taught in a manner relevant to the most crucial needs and concerns of students, teachers, and parents.

Among the skills emphasized in the study of economics are:

1. Becoming acquainted with modern economic theories and principles
2. Understanding how goods and services are produced, procured, and consumed
3. Understanding how time and resources can be allocated for the solution of economic problems
4. Reading economic barometers and extrapolating from them
5. Locating and using data on economic conditions and activities
6. Generating alternative solutions to personal economic problems

How Social Science Is Taught

Community Studies

Community studies can be taught in a number of ways, ranging from reading and recitation to making in-the-field case studies of different types of communities. Pupils' understanding of their communities can be encouraged and their skill in social analysis can be developed by setting up situations in which they talk with civic leaders and representatives of business and labor groups; by arranging trips to centers of community activity; and by promoting dramatic play, role-playing, and games involving decision-making.

Community studies lend themselves well to the use of multiphasic and multiperspective analyses, as well as a holistic synthesis of concepts, principles, and ideas from the several disciplines of the social sciences. To see clearly and to conceptualize the nature of interrelated communities, students should gain some facility in thinking like an historian, a political scientist, a psychologist, a sociologist, or an economist. This notion is treated in greater depth later in this chapter.

American History

World history has, to a large extent, a biographical base, which can be used as a frame of reference in the teaching of

American history. The record of the past need not be a lifeless recounting of details, dates, wars, and names. As told by a masterful storyteller, such as Thucydides, Shakespeare, or Churchill, history possesses all the flesh and blood and vigor of man coping with his environment and his fellow man.

History can also be taught as a source of knowledge and as a context for developing skills which man needs in order to appraise, criticize, and endorse. Two of these skills, analysis and evaluation, are used to discover which facts, events, and ideas are significant as guides to action or self-understanding. These skills may be used in assessing cause and effect and man's progress, lack of progress, or, in some instances, regression over recorded time.

American history is often taught as an interweaving series of stories, as a chronological listing of verified facts, and as a series of situations open to scrutiny and criticism. It is taught in a manner that emphasizes learning the facts necessary to succeed academically. It is also taught in ways that emphasize human development through growth in the skills of perceiving, relating, evaluating, analyzing, and formulating.

American Government

The subject of American government is usually taught in civics and government courses. In class discussions of values, points of view, and various patterns of action, students can develop their conceptions of fair play and due process of law. We teach American government indirectly by demonstrating our respect for all human rights and freedoms, and by exhibiting traits of leadership and fellowship that enhance rather than demean individuals.

One approach in teaching American government might be referred to as the *historical mode,* in which the learner gains skill in asking heuristic questions. He uses such questions to verify the authenticity of records, to establish the time and geographical position of events, and to make some judgments about the significance of those events.[3]

Another approach might be referred to as the *scientific,* or *political science, mode.* This mode of thinking about American government (1) engages the learner in thorough scrutiny, analysis, and interpretation of government programs and administration, with an emphasis upon inductive thinking, or (2) asks him to consider governmental structures as they exist in our society and to trace their development. The student

---

3. See Millard Clements, "Chapter III. The Disciplines and Social Study," *Effective Thinking In the Social Studies,* Jean Fair and Fannie R. Shaftel, eds. 37th Yearbook, National Council for the Social Studies (Washington: National Education Association, 1967), p. 60.

focuses primarily upon the processes involved in formulating, passing, and carrying out legislation, and learns about how the legality of laws and administrative acts are tested. He may also be asked to analyze relationships that exist among these functions and among persons who carry them out.

Economics

The teaching of economics has moved away from the presentation of abstract, formal theory alone, and is now related far more to everyday life. The current emphasis is upon how individuals and governments fill basic human needs and wants, and upon actions necessary to raise the standard of living of the human population.

Economics courses are relating theory to reality more and more through the use of case studies and simulations, or games. In addition, educators are reinforcing students' economic understanding by weaving certain economic concepts into other aspects of the curriculum and of student life, and thereby encouraging extrapolation.

Gauging Pupil Growth and Effectiveness

Acquisition and comprehension of basic facts in the social sciences may be determined with paper-and-pencil tests. Ratings can also be made on the basis of observation of change and growth: in pupils' attitudes toward others, in comprehension of the forces that cause events, in the skills of leading groups, and in active participation in various volunteer activities. Aids for such observation are teacher-designed checklists and rating sheets that show those traits and behaviors thought to characterize effective growth in the various social sciences.

A Holistic Approach to the Study of Man

Who is man? What has he achieved? What might he become? These questions from the beginning of the chapter are fundamental to research in the separate social sciences. They are questions to use in appraising the total curriculum and in attempting to define man in all aspects of his being.

In the classroom, integrated studies and multidisciplinary learning are needed for students to fully understand these questions. As separate studies, the social sciences analyze particular areas of human behavior, and are convenient structures to use in organizing and comprehending concepts and generalizations. But after dissecting man and his social behavior, it is necessary to put him together again. As in the case of Humpty Dumpty, the task is not easy; but it is possible that we can today work toward achieving a new synthesis, even a new image of man, using our knowledge of what man has been and what he might become.

A strategic place in which to effect a synthesis of the various social science disciplines might be the area of community studies. For example, students can study expanding geographical and political communities, and then analyze and relate the sociological, psychological, and economic components of their lives. They can then demonstrate their comprehension of a holistic approach by formulating and examining multiple explanations and solutions for a host of social problems and phenomena. With this experience, students are in a better position to understand the nature of man, and can perhaps better envision methods of achieving a more harmonious and productive existence.

Academic Skills

Examples of academic skill behavioral objectives are given for each of the social sciences.

Community Studies

1. Students are to develop understanding of the importance of volunteer services in improving the natural beauty, emergency services, or political participation of a community. Realization of this objective is to be judged by reference to the number of times a pupil volunteers to perform one of these functions, or to take courses to prepare to carry out these functions, and the amount of time he spends in performing them. When opportunities of the community permit, each pupil is to participate in at least one volunteer service activity during the school year.

2. Each student is to state his philosophy of life and personal code, including a set of values by which he plans to guide his behavior when with other persons in various situations. This statement is to be a written assignment consisting of no more than 700 words. The definitions of philosophy of life and personal code are to be developed and agreed upon by the teacher and a majority of the children in the class. The philosophy and personal code is to be evaluated on the basis of clarity of expression, consistency of ideas, and usefulness as a guide for behavior.

American History

1. The pupil completes a matching quiz, identifying with no more than one error the author or authors of: The Declaration of Independence, "Poor Richard's Almanac," "The Emancipation Proclamation," and "The Federalist Papers."
2. The pupil sets in proper time sequence six major events in American history on a teacher-prepared list.
3. The student develops a set of three criteria for distinguishing an event as "significant." He prepares a fifty-page notebook containing newspaper and magazine articles on national events occurring over a three-month period. He then (a) indicates which events will probably be included in high-school American history books in five years, (b) substantiates his choice of events, and (c) explains how the events meet his criteria for significance. This learning objective will be evaluated with standards established by the teacher and students regarding the appropriateness of the criteria, the effectiveness of the criteria when applied to the articles, and the credibility of the substantiation.
4. After studying research techniques used by historians, the pupil lists correctly three techniques for establishing the authenticity and approximate age of a document.

American Government

1. Within a three-minute period, the pupil tells his teacher three rights guaranteed by the first ten amendments to the U.S. Constitution.
2. In an oral or written presentation, the student explains why it is necessary to have a national government. His explanation should include at least three reasons and should refer to relationships among nations, states, and persons.
3. The student is to identify in a matching test the correct descriptions of at least seven of the following: Articles of Confederation, Bill of Rights, "Separation of Powers," "Judicial Review," "Four Freedoms," Marshall Plan, United Nations, SEATO, NATO, OAS, and CIA.

Economics

1. Playing the roles of customers and storekeepers, kindergarteners and first-graders dramatize situations showing that (a) the amount of money they have limits the number and kinds of items they can buy, and (b) that there may not be enough of a certain item for everyone to purchase it.
2. Using library reference books, eighty percent of the class prepare short written descriptions of eight or more of the following terms or names: mercantilism, laissez-faire,

capitalism, socialism, communism, *The Wealth of Nations,* cybernetics, NAM, CIO, A F of L, Reverend Thomas Malthus, John Stuart Mill, and Karl Marx.

Higher Cognitive Skills

Examples of behavioral objectives at this level are given for each area of the social sciences. Each skill is identified following the statement of the objective.

Community Studies

1. After a discussion of the goals, types of organization, and functions of communities, ninety percent of a group of third-grade children are able to tell in their own words what a community is. *(Interpretation)*
2. Following a discussion of the subject, students are to list three principles for keeping harmony in the home and neighborhood. They are then to indicate how these principles might be applied to relationships among states and among nations. *(Application)*
3. Students observe an affluent, an average, and a poor community and discern at least two examples of deprivation (parental, social, cultural, or nutritional) in each type of community. *(Analysis)*

American History

1. After studying the Civil War, fifth-grade students are to list political, economic, and social causes of the war. They are then to explain in their own words which, in their judgment, was the main cause of the war. Satisfactory completion of this assignment will be indicated when a pupil lists two of each type of cause and presents a statement of the main cause of the war that is logical in the judgment of the teacher. *(Interpretation and evaluation)*
2. Students are to read (a) a biography of John Adams, (b) a historical novel in which references are made to John Adams, (c) pages or chapters referring to Adams in a history of American political thought, (d) references to Adams in an economic history of the United States, and (e) references to Adams in an encyclopedia. They are then to prepare a 1500-word statement combining three or more perspectives on the man and on the period of American history in which he lived. *(Synthesis)*

American Government

1. In writing to a pen pal in another country, the pupil explains his feeling about the American flag, the national anthem, the President of the United States, and the role of the United States in world affairs. The letter should be written in a friendly, informal style and convey to the reader the personal feelings of the writer. *(Interpretation)*
2. Students select criteria and then compare the British and American systems of choosing, respectively, the prime minister and the president. They then prepare eight-minute speeches describing the relative strengths and weaknesses of each system. *(Analysis, synthesis, and evaluation)*

Economics

1. Students, provided with the necessary research skills, are to determine whether or not a laissez-faire policy with respect to governmental regulation of business resulted, during any period of American history, in a self-regulated and self-disciplined economic system operated in the best interests of all citizens. They are then to demonstrate that they have used three research skills in answering this question *(Analysis and evluation)*
2. Pupils are to make a mural illustrating five ways, discussed in textbooks and reference books, in which the invention of the automobile affected labor, consumers, and businessmen. *(Translation)*
3. To generate a number of possible principles to use in solving a management-labor dispute, students respond to the following question, "If government is to be fair to both labor and management, by what principles should it abide in ending a strike?" Students should list at least five principles judged practical by the teacher. *(Extrapolation)*

Practice. Having studied several examples of higher cognitive-skill behavioral objectives, the reader may be ready to follow these steps in preparing objectives that foster each of the major goals or skills outlined in the *Taxonomy:*

1. Decide upon a grade level or grade-level range.
2. Prepare a working definition of each of the higher cognitive skills in the *Taxonomy.*
3. Write on cards social-science behavioral objectives designed to foster development of each of the higher cognitive skills.
4. Have a co-worker review your behavioral objectives and then add the cards to your file.

Creative Skills

Examples of creative-skill behavioral objectives for each area of the social sciences follow. Each skill is identified following the statement of objective.

Community

1. To demonstrate his comprehension of principles of community living and government, and to demonstrate ability in creating solutions to current community problems, the student is to prepare a written plan of a model community in which (a) all people would live in harmony; (b) there would be no pollution of the environment; (c) there would be no traffic congestion; (d) all people would be healthy.

    Students fulfilling this objective satisfactorily should (a) deal with at least five principles of community living and government, and (b) have their plan judged original by a panel consisting of the teacher, a city official, and a representative of a local service club. *(Originality)*

2. Each student is to write a poem about what he likes or dislikes in his home, school, and community. The poem should identify at least three reasons for his likes or dislikes and should conclude with words which, in the opinion of the English teacher, show a feeling of civic responsibility. *(Fluency)*

American Government

1. After a study of American government and after using reference books for background material, students design a game for two or more persons (seventh-graders or adults) which involves a series of economic, political, and social decisions that an American citizen may make in his personal life and in his relationships with local, state, and national governments. *(Originality)*

2. Students think of different ways in which the American system of government could be improved. They do this in a divergent-production or brainstorming session in which judgment of responses is withheld. Eighty percent of the persons in the class should have five or more suggestions. *(Fluency)*

Economics

1. A group of five students is to prepare and act out three skits showing how a president or manager of a railroad might

conduct a business meeting under (a) a laissez-faire government, (b) capitalism, and (c) communism. The skits should incorporate facts and understandings acquired in a ninth-grade unit on economics. *(Flexibility)*

2. Pupils in the fifth grade are to take a toy designed for a younger child and think of ways to improve the toy and make it more marketable. They are then to prepare a report with illustrations showing their proposals. Three or more basic ways of improving the toy should be suggested by forty percent of the class. *(Flexibility)*

Leadership Skills

In addition to skill in motivating others, leadership skills include planning activities, organizing and coordinating the efforts of other persons, protecting members of a group, and evaluating the performance of the group and its individual members. Examples of behavioral objectives in leadership within the context of community studies follow:

1. Following a study of the local community, officers of a high-school senior class organize, direct, and evaluate a "Good-Turn Saturday," which is to be judged successful if seventy percent of the senior class participates in this community-service activity.

2. In a dramatic play of life in a frontier community, fifth-grade pupils take the roles of mayor, sheriff, councilmen, and other community leaders. Another group of fifth-grade pupils assume the roles of mayor of their present-day community, the chief of police, a health officer, councilmen, and other leaders. Both groups deal with the same basic problems in different manners. After this activity, nine out of ten students tell three or more principles of community government they have learned.

Discussion Questions and Activities

1. What are the social sciences? What do they have in common? How do they differ?

2. Why is each of the following taught: American government, American history, and economics?

3. Why is it important to stress holistic studies of man? How can this be accomplished?

4. In what ways might social science courses emphasize objectives listed in the *Taxonomy of Educational Objectives — Handbook II: Affective Domain?*

5. What benefits might accrue to the learner from inquiry and cognitive-process approaches to the various social sciences?

6. How might behavioral objectives in the social sciences and in English be mutually reinforcing? Give examples.

7. Hold a brainstorming session in a small group on the best ways of evaluating pupil growth and effectiveness in social science skills.

8. What problems might arise in the preparation of social science objectives? How might they be resolved?

9. How do students respond to behavioral goals and to a behavioral orientation to assignments?

Bibliography

American Association for the Advancement of Science. *Science—A Process Approach.* Chart. New York: Xerox, 1967.

Anderson, Harold H. *Creativity and Its Cultivation.* New York: Harper & Row, 1959.

Barnard, Chester. *Functions of the Executive,* 2nd ed. Cambridge: Harvard Univ. Press, 1968.

Bloom, Benjamin, et al. *Taxonomy of Educational Objectives,* Handbook I: *Cognitive Domain.* New York: McKay, 1956.

Brandwein, Paul F., et al. *The Social Sciences: Concepts and Values, K–6.* New York: Harcourt, Brace & World, 1970.

Bruner, Jerome. *The Process of Education.* Cambridge: Harvard Univ. Press, 1966.

California State Curriculum Commission. *Social Studies Framework for the Public Schools of California.* Sacramento: California State Department of Education, 1962.

Carpenter, Helen McCracken, ed. *Skill Development in Social Studies,* 33rd Yearbook, National Council for the Social Studies. Washington: National Education Association, 1963.

Cook, Desmond. "Program Evaluation and Review Technique—Applications in Education." Washington: U.S. Government Printing Office, 1966.

Fair, Jean, and Shaftel, Fannie R., eds. *Effective Thinking in the Social Studies,* 37th Yearbook, National Council for the Social Studies. Washington: National Education Association, 1967.

Gowan, John Curtis; Demos, George D.; and Torrance, E. Paul, eds. *Creativity: Its Educational Implications.* New York: Wiley, 1967.

Guilford, J. P. "Creativity: Its Measurement and Development," *A Source Book for Creative Thinking.* Edited by Sidney J. Parnes and Harold F. Harding. New York: Scribner's, 1962.

Iredell, Vernon R. "Methods of Inquiry," *The Social Sciences: Foundations of the Social Studies.* Edited by John U. Michaelis and A. Montgomery Johnston. Boston: Allyn & Bacon, 1965.

Krathwohl, David R., et al. *Taxonomy of Educational Objectives,* Handbook II: *Affective Domain.* New York: McKay, 1964.

LaRue, Sydney, and LaRue, William T. "Voices of Life" series. San Francisco: Century Communications, 1969 and 1970.

Lenz, Margaret, and Moss, Penrod. *What is Man?: Problems for Research: What is Man?: Findings from Research.* Newport Beach, Calif.: Franklin Publications, 1969.

McCune, George H., and Morse, Horace T., eds. *Selected Items for Testing of Study Skills and Critical Thinking,* rev. ed. Washington, D.C.: National Council for the Social Studies, 1964.

Meeker, Mary Nacol. *The Structure of Intellect—Its Interpretation and Uses.* Columbus, Ohio: Charles E. Merrill, 1969.

Michaelis, John U., and Johnston, A. Montgomery, eds. *The Social Sciences: Foundations of the Social Studies.* Boston: Allyn & Bacon, 1965.

Plowman, Paul D. "Encouraging the Development of the Talented in Academic Areas," *Education* 88, no. 1 (September–October 1967): 35–42.

Sanders, Norris. *Classroom Questions—What Kinds?* New York: Harper & Row, 1966.

Torrance, E. Paul. *Guiding Creative Talent.* Englewood Cliffs, N.J.: Prentice-Hall, 1962.

Wallas, Graham. *The Art of Thought.* New York: Harcourt, Brace, 1926.

Watson, Jane Werner. *Sciences of Mankind.* New York: Golden Press, 1960.

Williams, Frank E. *Workshops of the Use and Adaptation of New Media for Developing Creativity.* Washington: U.S. Dept. of Health, Education and Welfare, April 1968.

Winnetka Board of Education. *Supplement to the Social Studies Curriculum Guide.* Winnetka, Ill.: Winnetka Public Schools, 1967.

CHAPTER 5

MATHEMATICS

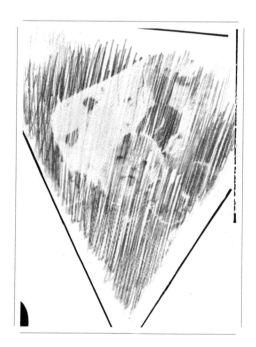

5

Mathematics in the Classroom

Academic Skills

Higher Cognitive Skills

Creative Skills

Mathematics is a symbolic language and a series of operations for use in describing relationships, solving problems, or predicting outcomes. As such, it is a means by which man records his possessions and profits and grapples with consumer, business, and scientific problems. Man leaves his imprint on chalkboards and computers and through these extensions of his mind explores alternative courses of action. Time saved by mathematically testing alternatives can be used to shorten the interval between hypothesis and discovery. Through the use of electronic computers, man simulates and tests economic and military conditions, charting his way to exceedingly complex decisions.

Mathematics was used by ancient Egyptians to account for grain in storehouses, to reestablish boundaries of farms after annual floods of water and alluvial mud, and to erect remarkably precise pyramids. It was used by ancient Greeks to explore the nature of numbers and to discover a system of mathematics called geometry. From early Babylonian times until today, work done in mathematics has enabled man to move with assurance across the face of the earth, on land, sea, and finally through the air and outer space.

Major developments in mathematics include the formulations of geometry, trigonometry, logarithms, calculus, theories of probability, non-Euclidean geometry, and theories of relativity. Building upon these, the twentieth century has become an age of research and development. During this time, pure mathematics has expanded through inclusion of functional analysis, topology, general theories of integration, and abstract algebra. Applications of mathematics are found in the formulation of mathematical models for interpreting parameters of our economic system and in the use of statistics and probability to forecast the results of presidential elections and the outcome of military strategy. Other diverse applications include guiding spacecraft and missiles; keeping track of buying and selling transactions on the stock exchange; predicting weather conditions; identifying criminals; making airline reservations; and monitoring the reports of American taxpayers.

Today, cyberneticians are linking computers and self-correcting automated means of production in ways that will greatly increase the nation's productivity. In fact, it is now predicted that within twenty to twenty-five years, ninety percent of our consumer goods will be produced by only ten percent of the adult working population. If this prognostication is realized, mathematics and modern technology will have created leisure that man may use to effect his ultimate fulfillment or his utter degradation. Despite minor aberrations, the tendency appears to be in the direction of full development of human potential.

Modern mathematics emphasizes logical, forceful, convergent thinking. It suggests a new discipline of the mind and of the will. It also emphasizes pure and applied thought that results in an extension of both man's knowledge and his power. Not to be overlooked are the esthetic aspects of pure mathematics, with applications in architecture and painting. Today it is opening up a new age of creativity, precision, and reason.

Mathematics in the Classroom

Why Mathematics Is Taught

Mathematics is taught in order to extend the learner's powers of communication and to enhance his skills of describing, calculating, resolving, and proving. Mathematics is taught as a means of increasing a person's effectiveness in his chosen profession and as an informed consumer. It is hoped that a knowledge of mathematics will give the student another means of ordering his world and of perfecting the society in which he lives.

What Is Taught in Mathematics and When It Is Taught

The content of mathematics instruction is undergoing significant changes. At one time the manipulation of logarithms (multiplying and dividing by adding and subtracting exponents) and triangulation aspects of trigonometry (using trigonometric tables that were merely extensions of those initiated by the early Greeks) were main aspects of study, but today these have been largely replaced, or at least obscured, by calculating devices and by the use of trigonometric functions to solve algebraic equations. Not only has the content changed, but so, too, has the "when" of mathematics instruction. Calculus, once encountered only in the university, is now taught in high school, and has become a requirement for admission to certain institutions of technology and science. Logic, once the domain of the college, is now taught to intellectually gifted pupils in the fourth grade.

The trend, however, is not just to teach mathematics at an earlier age, but rather to offer it at a time and in a sequence of experience that facilitates optimum learning. By relating mathematics to developmental aspects of learning and to developmental needs of children, educators may make mathematics an intriguing area of study for improving communication and the skills needed to solve economic, social, and political problems.

What is taught and what is learned in mathematics, as in other fields, might be reduced to certain elements, structures, and operations. *Elements,* of course, include number concepts and symbols. *Structures* are organized elements such as equations, graphs, tables, systems, and sets. *Operations* to be developed include: counting, measuring, adding, subtracting, multiplying, dividing, comparing, relating, solving, and predicting. Closely related to these operations or skills are the higher cognitive skills of interpreting, translating, extrapolating, applying, synthesizing, and evaluating.

How Mathematics Is Taught

In recent years, teaching methodologies regarding the introduction of concepts, the development of sequential skills, and the fostering of inquiry and creative production have been subjected to intensive research. From this research have followed developmental activities and products that purport to point the way toward increasing acquisition of essential knowledge (concepts, generalizations, principles, operations, and systems) and of sophisticated skills and operations. It would be foolhardy and presumptive to attempt to encapsulate all pertinent developments in this chapter. Some observations about the teaching of mathematics can be made without pretending to portray all that is significant in the area of teaching methodology in mathematics.

Characteristics of modern mathematics include: testing and challenging rules, principles, and descriptions of relationships; examining the basic rationale and structure of mathematical systems; and seeing the relevance of non-Euclidean geometry, game theory, unified-field theory, topology, probability theory, set theory, and statistics. Emphasis is also placed upon computer-assisted instruction and information-processing machines; unifying themes and strands; programed instruction; and precise statements, terminology, and symbols.

These esoteric and relatively new aspects of mathematics may be as exhilarating to the novitiate as to the experienced educator. But a discussion of how to teach a subject must deal not only with innovations but also with the basic nature of how teachers teach and how children learn.

For the learner, direct experiences in seeing, touching, and hearing are requisite to the development of abstract thought. They are necessary precursors to understanding mathematical concepts and to correctly applying mathematical skills. Through these experiences the child becomes able to note similarities and dissimilarities in sizes, amounts, and shapes; to orient himself in space; to perceive directionality and to habitualize his movements in writing, reading, and visualizing symbols and equations; to perform and compare operations and processes; and to perceive figure-ground and unified-field relationships.

As these statements imply, there is a need for teachers to capitalize on the motivational aspects of multi-media instruction as well as upon exploratory and experimental experiences. Undergirding these comments is the clear recognition that most persons learn better through seeing than through hearing — and still better through doing something that involves both seeing and hearing.

Not to be overlooked, especially for some children, are kinesthetic approaches to recognizing, internalizing, and then learning how to use symbols and shapes. Through his fingers, a child learns differences between symbols, solid things, and mathematical terms. As a result of holding such models as solid wooden pyramids, cubes, trapezoids, and rods, he gets some idea of how they differ and of relationships each might have to the others.

In the past, instruction in mathematics stressed memorization of facts and formulas, ability to apply facts and formulas in new settings, and analysis of written mathematical word problems. Today there appears to be greater attention directed toward discovery, personalized ways of perceiving and knowing, and exploration of alternative ways of solving problems or of describing things with mathematical terms and symbols. Also evident is a greater emphasis upon the skills of interpretation, translation, and extrapolation, as well as upon formulation of new principles and relationships among mathematical concepts. Important, too, has been the development of skills of evaluation and of ability and predilection to speculate.

Through discovery methods, we can traverse the mental terrain of spatial relations, of geometric forms in the everyday natural and man-made world. By applying discovery methods the teacher can help the student to comprehend proportion, size, comparisons, and relationships. As a result of these methods, the student learns to comprehend principles in new ways and fit elements together in systems or designs.

As a point of departure in methodology and as a matter of strategy, it is important for teachers to recognize the cumulative aspects of skill development in moving up a hierarchy of intellectual skills from cognition-memory through comprehension and on to analysis, synthesis, and evaluation. It is just as important to be ready to reverse the process for children unable to operate successfully at a particular level and to return their study to simpler levels of the hierarchy.

Teachers who wish greater acquaintance with ways of ordering content and skill acquisition might study exemplary curriculum guides, state frameworks, mathematics continuums, and programed instruction materials, some of which are included in the bibliography for this chapter.

Not to be overlooked as sources of guidance in teaching mathematics are the developmental psychology of Piaget and materials based upon the Cognitive Domain of the *Taxonomy of Educational Objectives*.

Gauging Pupil Growth and Effectiveness

Indications of effectiveness and growth in mathematics may be:

1. A child's improved ability to communicate, using mathematical terms and symbols
2. His speed and accuracy in performing operations or series of operations
3. His increased ordering of his world, dealing with it in a logical, precise, and rational manner
4. His growing interest in avocational and vocational aspects of mathematics

Other measures of the pupil's advancement are standardized tests of mathematical knowledge, understandings, and skills, teacher observation of mathematical problem-solving in informal and formal settings, and applications of mathematics in research projects in chemistry and physics. Growth can be seen by noting a child's current status in mastering hierarchical sequences and systems of skills. It can also be observed in the degree to which a child becomes increasingly interested in both the theoretical and esthetic aspects of mathematics. Especially helpful in the matter of assessment are efforts in recent years to (1) create programs of sequential concept and skill development and (2) prepare teachers to use these effectively.

Review of Procedures

In a sense, both mathematics and reading are natural domains for the development of performance skills. Both emphasize the use of abstractions in communicating, describing, and solving problems. Both require sequential skill and concept development. These fields are ones in which teachers may function as diagnosticians and prescription experts. The technical aspects of these roles do not in any way demean the role of the professional educator or teacher. Coordinated concept and skill development in individuals requires a high degree of artistry as well as practical classroom management.

When dealing with a student, we must attend to his specific motivations as well as to his background and current skill development in mathematics. Behavioral objectives need to be formulated for, modified for, and tailored to the needs of individuals. Sometimes this can be accomplished within the structure and process of established programs. At other times, the teacher himself must formulate objectives or experiences that will meet a child's particular need to master a concept or a skill, or that will develop the unique and possibly creative ways in which the child structures and manipulates the elements of mathematics.

With this in mind, a review of certain aspects of developing behavioral objectives might be helpful:

1. Define the term *behavioral objective*.
2. List four features that characterize this type of objective.
3. Which of the following objectives contain a clear description of behavior, mediating conditions, and levels of proficiency?

   a. First-grade children are to become familiar with the following symbols: (+), (−), (=), (×), (<), and (>).
   b. Students write a list of decimal numerals in expanded form using powers of the number 10. For example: $371 = (3 \cdot 10^2) + (7 \cdot 10^1) + (1 \cdot 10^0)$.
   c. Students illustrate the following statement: If the last digit of a decimal numeral is either five or zero, it is divisible by five.
   d. Following a reading assignment of the history of linear measurement, six out of ten students are able to present two arguments for and against the use of standard units of measurement and for and against the use of nonstandard units of measurement.
   e. Students are to find the length of one side of a right triangle when they are given the length of the other side

and of the hypotenuse. They are to show in class how they derived the answer. In checking the answers, the teacher should find that eighty percent of the students make no errors in either the answer or computations.

f. Fifth-grade pupils are to write the reciprocals of $\frac{1}{2}$, $\frac{1}{4}$, and 5 correctly within one minute.

g. Given a list of eleven numbers, students are to find the mean, the median, and the mode.

Which of the above objectives meets the requirements of behavioral objectives? If you analyze each objective carefully, you will see that objective e alone contains all the necessary parts of a well-written objective. Remember that those that can be classified as behavioral objectives contain: (1) a precise description of the behavior or performance; (2) conditions affecting performance or conditions under which performance may be observed, tested, or judged; (3) expected level of proficiency; and (4) means for judging whether or not the student can perform or behave at an established level of proficiency.

Now write out those parts of objective e that match this list of elements of good objectives. If possible, compare your responses with those made by co-workers in your school or school district. Are your responses similar or different? If different, why? Is there room for some differences in interpretation?

As a matter of review it might be advisable to state again the steps in framing behavioral objectives:

A. Determine precisely what you want a student to do.
B. Establish facilitating or limiting conditions that will affect performance of the task.
C. State expected proficiency levels or standards to be met.
D. Decide which procedures to use in judging whether or not the expected level of skill has been attained.
E. Incorporate items 1 through 4 in a coherent statement.

By now you may have noticed the tendency of behavioral objectives to be longer than other objectives. Try to resist this tendency and make statements as succinct as possible.

4. Using the code B, C, P, and M, indicate which of the distinguishing features are contained in and which are missing from statements a, b, c, d, f, and g in question 3. Set up your answer in this format:

Elements and Features Present	Elements and Features Missing

After you have completed this task, compare your answers with those of co-workers. Then check your answers with those given on page 95.

5. As a final task, select three of the previous statements (a, b, c, d, f, and g). Rewrite them to incorporate missing elements or characteristics.

Based on the experience of previous chapters, as well as the review just accomplished, behavioral objectives in mathematics — academic, higher cognitive, and creative skill — should now be considered. Bear in mind that it is quite natural to have some overlap in objectives that form part of a cumulative hierarchy in which skills lower in the hierarchy are both a part of and necessary antecedents of higher cognitive skills. Then, too, there exists an intimate relationship between certain traits of creativity and certain higher cognitive skills that are thought to be earmarks of intelligence. Fluency, flexibility, awareness, and sensitivity have a direct impact on man's rationality or potential for intelligent behavior. Productive divergent thinking, the generation of numerous alternatives or solutions, is dependent upon attitudes and processes for extending awareness, for overcoming obstacles to thinking and doing, and for creating original and useful products.

Academic Skills

Because of the vast body of mathematical knowledge, it will be necessary to be highly selective in the choice of illustrations and topics. Behavioral objectives in history of mathematics, terms and symbols, operations involving whole numbers, measurement, equations, and graphs will cover only a portion of the academic skills in mathematics.

History of Mathematics

1. After a study of the mathematics used by the Babylonians, Chinese, and Egyptians as early as 3000 B.C., fourth-grade pupils are to make murals or to prepare twenty-page notebooks illustrating numeration systems, arithmetical operations, and geometry used by these ancient peoples in business, engineering, and government. Eight out of ten pupils completing this assignment should receive a satisfactory rating from a panel of three teachers for accuracy of information, effective composition, organization, clarity, and creativity.

2. Students are to read a book on the history of mathematics and then prepare a panel discussion on five important developments in mathematics in the past fifty years. The panel is to be chosen by the class. Each panelist will be given eight minutes for an initial presentation and will be judged on his presentation and on his asking and responding to questions.

3. To acquire an understanding of systems of mathematics developed independently by two persons, high-school seniors are to study the work of Baron Wilhelm von Leibniz and Sir Isaac Newton in discovering the principles of calculus, and the work of Nikolai Lobachevski and Janos Bolyai in discovering some of the noneuclidean systems of geometry. The latter should be compared with the later work of Georg Riemann in the same field. This study should include the reading of reference and biographical material and should be summarized in a 1000-word composition.

Terms and Symbols

1. Fourth-grade pupils are to demonstrate their understanding of terminology associated with properties of operations by (a) defining *commutative property, associative property,* and *distributive property;* and (b) identifying from a list of equations appropriate illustrations of each property. Four out of five pupils in the class should define the three terms correctly and make no more than one error in associating illustrations with the properties.

2. In an ungraded primary classroom, pupils are to demonstrate to the teacher's satisfaction their understanding of the following terms: *inch, foot,* and *year; o'clock; value* and *worth; minute, hour, day,* and *month; cup, pint, quart,* and *gallon; pound; line, line segment,* and *end point; number* and *number sentence; add, multiply, subtract,* and *divide;* and *dozen.* The ways in which pupils will demonstrate their understanding will include carrying out certain mathematical operations using appropriate measuring instruments, matching pairs of cards that contain the term and the definition of the term, and defining terms orally or in writing.

3. Upon completing reading assignments and discussion, eighty percent of the sixth-grade class is to define in writing with no more than one error each of the following symbols: (π), (ν), $(\%)$, $(\approx)$, (η), and $(\overrightarrow{AB})$.

Operations Involving Whole Numbers

1. With the aid of a slide rule, eighth-grade students are to multiply ten sets of two-digit numbers chosen by the

teacher. Eighty percent of the students' answers are to be verified by the teacher as sufficiently accurate approximations.

2. After setting down the multiplication facts with nine as one factor, and arranging the products in order of increasing size, pupils are to interpret relationships they see (a) between the factor multiplied by nine and the first digit of the product, (b) between digits in the products, and (c) between the tens digits in the column of products. Each pupil is to note at least one relationship; eight out of ten pupils are to note two or more relationships. Responses may be written or oral.

Measurement

1. With a 100 cc graduate and a weight scale, pupils in a sixth-grade science class are to weigh fifty cc, sixty cc, seventy cc, and eighty cc of tap water. They are to record their results in grams and then are to deduce and record the weight of one cc of water. Weights are to be compared with the standard weight of one cc of water. This assignment is to be repeated with liquids of other densities. Eighty-five percent of the students should achieve the level of accuracy determined in advance by the teacher.
2. Using a meter stick, third-grade students are to measure the height of classmates, the dimensions of their desks, and the length and width of their classroom. Two or more students should get the same height for each classmate. All students should get approximations within eight centimeters of the actual length and width of the classroom.
3. To show their knowledge of measuring instruments, ninth-grade students are to match the names of the following instruments with descriptions of what they measure: (a) altimeter, (b) caliper, (c) chronometer, (d) galvanometer, (e) pedometer, (f) range finder, (g) sextant, (h) tachometer, (i) barometer, (j) transit, and (k) protractor. The descriptions of what the instruments measure are to be supplied by the teacher. Students should have no more than three errors in this assignment.

Equations

1. Following a lesson on multiplying binomials, ninety-five percent of the ninth-grade students get the correct trinomial when multiplying a teacher-selected binomial by itself.
2. Upon completing first-year algebra, ninth-grade students are to demonstrate to the satisfaction of their teacher that they can solve both linear and quadratic equations. The chalkboard or pencil and paper may be used.

3. Fourth-grade students are to study the commutative, associative, and identity properties of addition and multiplication. Each fourth-grade pupil should then be able to tell
which property is illustrated by each of nine equations on
a list prepared by the teacher. He should be able to do this
in five minutes with no more than one error.

Graphs

1. Following a discussion of graphs and the appropriateness
of certain types of graphs for different purposes or for
different types of data, seventh-grade students are given
four sets of data and are asked (a) to decide which set of
data is best represented by a bar graph, which by a picture
graph, which by a circle graph, and which by a line graph;
and (b) to plot each set of data on an appropriate graph.
Eighty-five percent of the class should complete this assignment and earn at least a grade of C.
2. To discover the practical application of graphs in the
transportation industry, eighth-grade students are to find or
make examples of graphs used to plot the speed traveled
and the time and duration of stops of truck drivers; weather
conditions; and the financial status of a railroad, trucking
firm, bus company, or airline. These graphs are to be
mounted in a notebook that tells the story of graphing.

Practice in Forming Behavioral Objectives

Prepare three academic behavioral objectives for children at
the grade level you teach for each of the following areas:

1. History of Mathematics
2. Terms and Symbols
3. Measurement
4. Equations
5. Graphs

These are to be put on cards and filed. Then try formulating
academic behavioral objectives for some of the areas not
covered, such as rational numbers and numeration systems.

After some experience in formulating behavioral objectives,
you may want to involve Future Teachers of America, interns,
teacher's aides, and selected bright students in attempts to
(1) develop behavioral objectives and (2) prepare a sequence
of instruction or a programed learning package for teaching
certain concepts and skills.

Higher Cognitive Skills

Behavioral objectives in mathematics can be formulated to develop various levels of higher cognitive skills. Examples follow, with indications of the cognitive skill involved:

1. Each member of a high school mathematics club is to apply correctly and accurately principles of measurement, geometry, or trigonometry in determining the dimensions of a playground, the cubic feet of air in a classroom or gymnasium, and the height of the tallest building on campus or in the community. Each member is to check the work and findings of at least two other members. Findings are to be verified as correct and accurate by the club sponsor or by authoritative documents such as architectural plans. *(Application)*

2. Without consulting any teacher, tenth-grade students are to determine which mathematical facts or operations can be used to solve problems in homemaking, manual training, biology, chemistry, or physics. They are to make charts showing in what subjects, for what purposes, and in what manners these facts and operations can be applied. These charts are to be presented to teachers of these subjects for their reaction and verification. Seventy-five percent of the charts are to be judged accurate by the teachers. *(Analysis)*

3. After a study of representation and misrepresentation of the economic health of a corporation, students are to read an annual report of a corporation and then determine (a) whether or not the corporation used the best type of graphs, tables, or charts to represent a particular body of economic data or to achieve a particular purpose of the person or business making the report; (b) whether the data was represented fairly to stockholders without business and accounting backgrounds; and (c) whether or not there was any misrepresentation in the graphic representation of statistical information. *(Evaluation)*

4. Ninth-grade students are to examine a mathematical word problem and to determine which elements are relevant to and needed in the solution of the problem. Relevant elements are defined as those that must be translated into equation form or used in arithematical operations to solve the problem. Eighty percent of the class should be in agreement as to what constitutes a relevant element. *(Evaluation and synthesis)*

5. To determine the fastest and the most accurate process for

finding the height of a seven-story structure, ninth-grade students and their teacher are to time and check the degree of accuracy of solutions derived by (a) using right triangles and trigonometry, (b) using proportion and the shadow of the structure and the shadow and known height of another object or structure, (c) measuring the height of one story and multiplying the result by seven, and (d) locating and consulting architectural plans. The findings of all students are to show a .86 correlation with the findings of the teacher. *(Evaluation)*

6. Following a study of certain mathematical discoveries, inventions, or "breakthroughs," eighty-five percent of fifth-grade students are to make reports judged convincing by the teacher and fifty percent of the class as to why certain of these discoveries might be considered more important than others. Substantiations might be in terms of social utility or in terms of contribution to basic knowledge and pure research. *(Evaluation)*

7. After studying mathematical terms and symbols, pupils are to interpret in their own words the meaning of five terms used in a mathematical statement and five symbols used in an equation. *(Interpretation)*

8. Students having access to reference materials and resource persons are to determine relationships existing between pairs of different mathematical terms, symbols, principles, operations, or processes. Relationships discovered or noted are to be described in a written report. *(Synthesis)*

9. Ninth-grade students are to use mathematical processes in solving personal or family problems, such as those involved in ordering lumber, in figuring how much cement is needed to make a mowing strip around a lawn, or in determining whether it is better to get a student loan at a bank, a credit union, or a savings and loan association. During a two-month period, three out of five students in the class are to relate at least two instances when they needed to use mathematics in their personal lives. *(Application)*

Creative Skills

Creative skill objectives might encompass and be directed toward a number of traits and competencies. Only three will be considered here: fluency, flexibility, and originality.

Fluency

With practice, pupils can move from pedestrian to quite rapid methods of computation, without loss of accuracy. As learning becomes more flexible and more playful, a child's fluency in mathematics may show itself in the production of unique methods of solving problems or describing relationships. Some behavioral objectives promoting fluency are:

1. A group of ten eighth-grade students is to read a book on high-speed computation. They are then to demonstrate speed and proficiency in competition with a group of students of equal ability who have not done the extra reading. Both groups are to solve a series of problems posed by the teacher, and the results are to be compared for speed and accuracy. Students in the first group are to do the problems in one-half the time with no sacrifice in accuracy.

2. Given practical problems of measuring or computing the circumference of a circle, the height of a flagpole, the volume of a water storage tank, the weight of a railroad flatcar loaded with coal, or the value of a certain common stock, students are to solve the problems rapidly by using computational shortcuts, a slide rule, and a calculator. The work of sixty-five percent of the students should be judged rapid and accurate by the teacher.

Flexibility

The ability to shift to different approaches, methods, or even different devices in solving problems may be to some degree an earmark of creativity. Students may gain speed through the use of different devices. Flexibility in the use of these devices and in the use of different ways of solving problems not only allows the student to select the device and the method most appropriate in a given situation but it also provides him with a means of checking solutions. Examples of behavioral objectives promoting flexibility are:

1. To demonstrate proficiency in solving problems in which (a) land area is described in square rods, acres, square miles, hectares, and square kilometers; and (b) liquid volume is described in U.S. gallons, imperial gallons, liters, British quarts, and U.S. quarts. This should be done by fifth-grade students who have studied conversion factors. Problems solved should show results in terms of two or more units of measurement.

2. High-school students engaged in solving problems with the aid of an electronic computer are to demonstrate ability to solve certain of these problems by hand or with

the aid of an electric but nonelectronic desk calculator. The problems are to be formulated by the teacher and are to be solved in a manner meriting a satisfactory rating for eighty-five percent of the students.

3. Following experiences with rounding off numbers and with using different ways of expressing results of a particular business transaction or industrial process, students are to show how they would express the same data in reports to accountants, to engineers, to consumers, and to stockholders. This assignment should be summarized in a 2000-word report containing at least four diagrams or charts. Five out of six students are to complete this assignment as homework during a two-week period.

Originality

The ability to synthesize knowledge in creating something new may be a key trait of individuals described as creative. Sometimes the creative product is the result of modification or of new applications. At other times, it may be startlingly novel, without apparently having been influenced by other ideas or events. While the latter may be exceedingly rare, such creative thoughts and acts do appear, even in children and young adults. Examples of behavioral objectives focusing on originality are:

1. Children are to design new ways of measuring distance, surface area, volume, weight, and speed. This assignment is to be completed after experiences in brainstorming and divergent thinking, and after acquaintance with other techniques used by industry to generate creative products. Three out of eight suggestions should be judged promising by the class and merit testing to determine accuracy, speed, and practicality.

2. Following a study of mathematical terminology and symbols, children are to suggest new symbols and terms that might help to clarify mathematical concepts or operations. From a class of twenty-five pupils should come seven or eight terms or symbols that are judged original by the teacher.

3. Given access to class reference materials and books in the public library, students are to write "You Are There" reports on one or more of the mathematical discoveries or inventions of Karl Gauss, Sir Isaac Newton, or Albert Einstein. The report is to be judged good by both an English and a mathematics teacher.

4. Students are to read an imaginative story incorporating elements of mathematical logic. They are then to write

comparable tales. The creative writings of two out of twenty students are to be considered good enough to merit distributing to two or more mathematics classes.

Discussion Questions and Activities

1. What are the basic mathematical elements, operations, and structures taught in elementary school and high school?

2. List five major mathematical developments of the past fifty years.

3. Describe five innovations in the teaching of mathematics that have been introduced in the past fifteen years.

4. How has the developmental psychology of Jean Piaget affected the teaching of mathematics to children?

5. Compose and write behavioral objectives in mathematics, emphasizing the following traits of creativity: fluency, flexibility, originality, and sensitivity to problems. Ask a friend or co-worker to make some judgments on the quality of the objectives you prepared.

6. Each teacher over the years acquires his own storehouse of workable techniques. These he uses with skill and effectiveness in attracting attention to a subject-matter area and in involving children in the mysteries and delights of content and skills. In a moment of altruism (why not now?), share one or more of these gems with a fellow teacher.

Answers to Review Question 4

Pages 86–87:

Elements and Features Present	Elements and Features Missing
a. -	a. B, C, P, M
b. B	b. C, P, M
c. B	c. C, P, M
d. B, C, P	d. M
f. B, C, P	f. M
g. B, C	g. P, M

Bibliography

Anastasiow, Nicholas, and Jerman, Max. *An Introduction to Computer-Based Drill and Practice in Arithmetic.* New York: L. W. Singer, 1968.

Arithmetic Teacher. Washington: National Council of Teachers of Mathematics. (All issues.)

Bereiter, Carl. *Arithmetic and Mathematics.* San Rafael, California: Dimensions Publishing Co., 1968.

Bergamini, David. *Mathematics.* Life Science Library. New York: Time, 1963.

Biggs, Edith E., and MacLean, James R. *Freedom to Learn: An Active Learning Approach to Mathematics.* Don Mills, Canada: Addison-Wesley, 1969.

California Statewide Mathematics Advisory Committee. *Mathematics Program, K–8.* Report to the California State Board of Education and the California State Curriculum Commission, 1968.

Center for the Study of Evaluation, Instructional Objectives Exchange. *Mathematics K–3; Mathematics 4–6; Mathematics 7–9.* Los Angeles: University of California, 1969.

Clark County School District. *Mathematics Curriculum Guide K–6.* Las Vegas: Clark County School District, 1967.

Denholm, Richard A.; Stiel, Edsel F.; and Blank, V. Dale. *Insight into School Mathematics.* Teacher's edition. Chicago: Science Research Associates, 1968.

Featherstone, Joseph. "The Primary School Revolution in Britain," *The New Republic* 157, nos. 8–9 (1967).

Frankl, Viktor E. *Man's Search for Meaning.* New York: Washington Square Press, 1963.

Glennon, Vincent J., and Callahan, Leroy G. *Elementary School Mathematics — A Guide to Current Research,* 3d ed. Washington, D.C.: Association for Supervision and Curriculum Development, 1968.

The Growth of Mathematical Ideas, Grades K–12. 24th Yearbook, National Council of Teachers of Mathematics, 1959.

Learning Research and Development Center, and Research for Better Schools, Inc. *Mathematics Continuum — Individually Prescribed Instruction.* Philadelphia: Research for Better Schools.

Los Angeles County Superintendent of Schools Office, Division of Elementary Education. *A Guide to Curriculum Development and Course of Study for Elementary Schools of Los Angeles County.* Los Angeles, 1965.

Mathematics Teacher. Washington: National Council of Teachers of Mathematics. (All issues.)

Minnesota State Department of Education. *Mathematics Flyer 13,* no. 1 (Fall 1968). Edited by David L. Dye.

Nuffield Mathematics Project. *Beginnings; Computation and Structure; Desk Calculators; I Do and I Understand; Pictorial Representation; Shape and Size; Your Child and Mathematics; Graphs Leading to Algebra; Environmental Geometry; Mathematics Begins; Probability and Statistics; Problems — Green Set.* New York: John Wiley, 1967 and 1968.

Polya, G. *How to Solve It.* Garden City, N.Y.: Doubleday, 1957.

Research for Better Schools, Inc. *Teaching In I.P.I. Mathematics,* a six-volume set. Philadelphia: Research for Better Schools, 1969.

Sharpe, Glyn H. *Some Behavioral Objectives for Elementary School Mathematics Programs.* Denver: Colorado State Department of Education, 1966.

Suppes, Patrick, and Hill, Shirley. *First Course in Mathematical Logic.* New York: Blaisdell, 1964.

Suppes, Patrick, and Jerman, Max. *Individualized Mathematics: Drill and Practice Kits.* New York: Singer, 1969.

Suppes, Patrick; Jerman, Max; and Brian, D. *Computer-Assisted Instruction at Stanford: The 1965–66 Arithmetic Drill-and-Practice Program.* New York: Academic Press, 1968.

Winnetka Board of Education. *Mathematics Curriculum Guide.* Winnetka, Ill.: Winnetka Public Schools, 1966.

CHAPTER 6

SCIENCE

6

The Nature of Science Education

Higher Cognitive Skills

Creative Skills

Craftsmanship Skills

Sample Behavioral Objectives

Science is man, method, product, and knowledge.
Science is a cricket chirping and a jet roaring
  — a child's curiosity and an old man's routines.
  — a flash of meteoric light and the abysmal darkness of an
  oceanic trench
Science is the dawn of man and his demise.
Science is phenomena.
Science is problem finding, defining, and solving
  — research and development.
Science is analysis, synthesis, and evaluation
  — the application of principles and explanations
Science is the wonder of intergalactic matter
  — and the birth of a baby.
Science is the certainty of springtime and fall, of sun and rain, of
  moon and stars.
Science is hot sulphuric acid and an ice-fed mountain stream
  — a placid ooze of green algae and the flashing tails of the
  piranha fish.
Science is a series of food chains and ecological progression.
Science is a ruby laser and an electronic computer
  — logical thinking and intuitive leaps.
Science is technology — production, processing, and monitor-
  ing; fabrication and creativity.
  Science is:
    tranquility and terror,
    fear and hope,
    speculation and fulfillment.
What is science?
  Again we say:
    Science is man
      — the scientist.
    Science is method
      — ways of discovering and knowing.
    Science is product
      — an electron microscope, a new car, an atomic
      pile.

Science is knowledge
— systematized and pursued for its own sake or to
solve a problem.

Man's story of scientific achievement is an exciting adventure of overcoming obstacles in his environment and in himself. Science has provided man with the methods, products, and knowledge needed to fashion a better world. As a creator of buildings, machines, and artificial human parts, man can now emancipate himself from old routines and old expectancies. He can use a portion of his power to free and remake himself. He can remake his environment and himself through logic and reason, and through intuition and speculation.

For what purposes has man created techniques of research and development, new modes of thought, and new ways of probing and responding? Certainly not just to refine his means of transportation and to improve the quality of his food. Then, for what purpose? Central to man's strivings in the last half of the twentieth century has been the motivation to improve himself—in all aspects of his being. This he may accomplish through discovery and application of tools and concepts in the behavioral, biological, and physical sciences.

The Nature of Science Education

What Is Taught

The knowledge content of science has been organized and is continually being reorganized in and among a host of "ologies," from archeology to zoology. The skill content of science has likewise been scrutinized and organized in various ways. A classic example of skill-content organization is what is termed *the scientific method.* For years students have been taught about and have been given experience in this method. Usually it starts with defining a problem, and then progresses through stages of generating possible solutions or explanations: observing, measuring, testing, and experimenting; organizing and interpreting data; forming conclusions; and communicating findings and conclusions to others.

Although the scientific method is helpful in portraying a logical and sequential approach to understanding the natural and physical world, it is not a method universally and consistently applied by all scientists. As a matter of fact, scientists often apply highly individualistic styles of inquiry and experimentation in solving problems and in arriving at explanations and conclusions. Because of the unique dynamics of inquiry, problem solving, and creativity, science educators have tended not to refer to *the* scientific method. Instead, they have focused upon acquiring multiple ways of perceiving, organizing, solving, and communicating. Science educators now stress the importance of developing proficiency in certain processes, in preparation for the time when these processes may be used in numerous combinations to strengthen man's quest for order, knowledge, and understanding.

One should not forget, however, that the word *method* generally means an established and accepted way of attaining a goal, or an organized set of processes or procedures for achieving a certain goal. In light of this definition, it would still seem appropriate to talk about the methods and methodologies of science, recognizing the dynamics of change in the constant restructuring of methods. Science itself can be viewed as a method of organizing knowledge and of finding out about man and everything his mind and eye perceive.

In science, the process skills (for example, gathering, analyzing, and interpreting data) are acquired most effectively through experiences that make sense to individuals and enhance their knowledge and intellectual power—experiences that can then lead to generalizations that those individuals have discovered and internalized.

If this is true, teachers must (1) plan exploratory experiences with concrete objects, theoretical models, and mathematical tools; (2) lead children step-by-step to the understanding of systematized knowledge; and (3) provide an experimental base for a child to use in organizing knowledge in rather unique and personally meaningful ways.

In writing behavioral objectives in science, a start can be made by using those skills that are described as essential to a particular scientific process or method. Some skills and processes that have been identified in recent years in lists and charts developed by science educators can be included as such starting points. Examples of such charts are the Costa and American Association for the Advancement of Science references included at the end of this Chapter.

In the area of science, we should teach and a child should learn basic concepts, principles, and ways of knowing. A child should acquire the attitudes and skills of scientific inquiry. In science, we should basically impart academic-content skills, steps in the creative process, higher intellectual skills, and certain craftsmanship skills. We should prepare a child to think inductively and deductively, and to make intuitive leaps from what is known or assumed to new insights, solutions, or explanations. Important, certainly, are techniques for (1) challenging a fact, a principle, a theory, or a law;

(2) using data from a number of disciplines in solving a problem; (3) building new structures of concepts, principles and goals; and (4) designing and using systems helpful in portraying and managing a process or series of steps in scientific inquiry and experimentation.

How Science Is Taught

We can now investigate the ways that science is being taught today, as well as how it might better be taught. Science is an exploration into the "how and why," the "what might happen if." It is an area of study in which we foster rigorous, analytical, convergent, problem-solving thinking as well as productive, divergent, creative thinking.

In the study of science a child learns how to interpret facts, functions, processes, and phenomena. He learns how to express them in concise terms, sometimes graphically or through mathematical expressions. He also learns how to formulate and apply hypotheses and principles, and how to evaluate a process, product, condition, or reaction.

When developing strategies for teaching science, teachers would do well to recognize the simple fact that they have taught only when children have learned. Learning requires a willingness on the part of the student to enter the teacher's world, to participate in activities, to accept knowledge, and, in general, to deal directly with the world; or it requires that the teacher enter the child's world as co-discoverer, creator, or learner. A third alternative is that of carefully setting the stage in which a child, independent of ostensible directions from the teacher, proceeds to inquire, to explain, and to comprehend.

A child learns principles of science by observing, inquiring, applying, testing, validating, analyzing, evaluating, and resolving. He learns the concepts, principles, generalizations, and skills of science through various teacher-contrived encounters with persons, books, materials, equipment, and environments. He learns through encounters with the biological and physical world.

Gauging Pupil Growth and Effectiveness

Science emphasizes a systematized approach to knowledge and ways of knowing, and growth in these areas is a clear indication of effectiveness and progress in science instruction. We can reasonably inquire into which concepts a student has mastered and into his level of comprehension. We can note his skill in asking questions, in formulating hypotheses, and in seeking reasonable and comprehensive explanations. Important, too, will be his ability to gather, organize, and interpret data; to formulate conclusions; and to communicate his findings to others. Teachers can gauge growth and effectiveness by observing, measuring, or testing a child's abilities in the following areas:

1. Factual knowledge.
2. Facility in such scientific processes as observing, measuring, organizing, interpreting, and communicating
3. Systematic approaches to organizing information, thinking rationally, making explanations, solving problems, and directing research efforts
4. Familiarity with and use of inductive, deductive, and intuitive methods in attempting to answer questions about the biological and physical world
5. Fluency, flexibility, originality, autonomy, persistence, and comprehension
6. Personal styles of inquiry, experimentation, problem solving, and idea generation
7. Interest in scientific hobbies or projects, or in scientific articles and books
8. Interest in an area or areas of science or in a scientific career
9. Original scientific products, such as equipment or devices, ideas, and explanations

Some of the most common ways of determining growth and effectiveness are through standardized tests and checklists or rating scales. These can determine the extent to which a student's answers to questions involve analysis, synthesis, and evaluation, or problem-solving and idea-generating thinking. Another method of evaluation is through observation—of the extent to which a student applies scientific knowledge, inquiry skills, problem-solving techniques, and experimentation when he is confronted with new problems and situations.

Counselors and teachers may have access to library records that show changes in students' reading patterns. Open-ended questions and autobiography assignments may also reveal the nature and extent of a child's interest in science as an area of study, as a subject in which to acquire certain transferable skills, or as a life career.

Objectives Concerning Man

To comprehend the nature, meaning, scope, and organization of science, we must understand man as a scientist—as a seeker, discoverer, and inventor, as an organizer and producer. Representative behavioral objectives highlighting *man* are:

1. After observing a television broadcast or film of astronauts in training, the student is to (a) design and use a spacecraft

simulator, or (b) prepare and take part in an eight-hour training program to acquire certain skills needed in manning a spacecraft. The spacecraft simulator or the training program is to be based upon existing spacecraft and astronaut-training programs. The student is to remain in the simulator for two hours and maintain voice contact with a "base" every five minutes. Improvement in five skills should be evidenced by the teacher's rating of the student before and after the training period.

2. Students are to develop a five-point rating scale and then rate ten twentieth-century scientists in terms of their discoveries, inventions, or ideas for improving the standard of living of the American people. Each student is to select one scientist that he considers to be the most outstanding and give reasons for his selection.

3. Students are to determine, through reading three or more books approved by the American Library Association, whether or not Aristotle's system of classifying seashells has had any effect upon current categories and nomenclature.

4. Students direct and produce five-minute recorded interviews with three scientists who enjoy art or music. They are to ask scientists the question, "Of what value is art or music to the scientist?"

Objectives Concerning Method

The choice of methods or methodologies of science is of utmost importance, for, to a large extent, solutions of problems and explanations of phenomena are determined by processes and procedures used in gathering, organizing, and interpreting data. Science students must become aware of and refine certain procedures and processes for conceptualizing problems, formulating hypotheses, gathering and organizing data, evaluating data, making inferences from data, forming conclusions, and communicating findings and conclusions. Students must be able to make intelligent choices of methods and processes to use in a given situation. Examples of behavioral objectives highlighting *method* follow:

1. *Defining a Problem.* To acquire some basis for further exploration, research, or study, students are to describe in 500-word written descriptions (a) damage done by the Japanese beetle, fire ant, mosquito, grasshopper, or field mouse in California, (b) obstacles to solving such a problem, and (c) unsuccessful attempts to eradicate the pests. Eighty percent of each description should be in words at a fifth-grade reading level. Twenty percent of the words may

be highly specialized scientific terms. Nine out of ten pupils should indicate that they understand the problem after reading each statement.

2. *Generating Hypotheses and Possible Solutions.* An hypothesis might be expressed to a young child by asking, "Just suppose we were troubled by mice, what could we do?" To an older child, the question might be phrased, "If this is the problem (or if these conditions exist), what might we do to solve it (or how might we deal with them)?" At this point, attempts to modify unsuccessful solutions or remedies might be helpful. Another approach would be to apply self-interrogation techniques, brainstorming procedures, or the creative process.[1] The latter should really include time scheduled for "incubation." Two behavioral objectives regarding generating hypotheses and possible solutions are:

a) Students are to develop and test alternative hypotheses to eliminate the Japanese beetle from California. This is to be done after students have studied the life cycle of the beetle and methods used to determine its presence. Then students are to prepare 1500-word reports with at least three illustrations of their findings, conclusions, and recommendations. Consideration should be given to the introduction of certain species of birds or insects to help eradicate the pest, the use of insecticides, and the development of a trapping system. Hypotheses and conclusions should be judged reasonable by a science teacher, 4-H club leader, county farm agent, or researcher for the U.S. Department of Agriculture.

b) Students are to give as many explanations as they can for a descriptive event featured in an "inquiry training film. A class of twenty-five students should yield at least six explanations for certain events or phenomena.

3. *Gathering Information and Data.* Students locate and record information from newspapers, scientific journals, state officials, and the U.S. Department of Agriculture on the influx or spread of the Japanese beetle, fire ant, grasshopper, mosquito, or field mouse in California. Data gathered from each source should be judged valid by a college science professor, librarian, or scientist working in the research laboratory of a chemical company.

1. See Graham Wallas, *The Art of Thought* (New York: Harcourt, Brace & World, 1926) and Alex F. Osborne, *Applied Imagination* (New York: Scribner's, 1957).

4. *Organizing and Interpreting Data.*

   a) Students use an outlining system for organizing major and minor points in preparing a written report on eradication of pests. Every member of the class is to prepare a report using major categories and first subcategories.

   b) Pupils write names of animals on cards and put them into the categories of mammals, birds, amphibians, reptiles, and insects. Young children or average students are to spell the common names correctly. Older students or college-bound students are to spell correctly both the common names and the scientific names of the animals.

   c) Students compare the beaks of fifteen birds observed in mountainous, desert, seashore, and meadow regions and indicate in a fifteen-page illustrated report the likely sources of food for each type of bird. The report should make clear to eighty percent of a class (grades five through eight) the relationship between structure of the beak and source of food. The percentage figure will be determined by a quiz in which children match names or pictures of five different types of beaks with names or pictures of five different sources of food.

5. *Formulating Conclusions.* After experimenting with different types of electrical switches, ninth-grade students will determine which type of switch might be used under different conditions and for different purposes. In a ten-minute period, students should describe at least four types of switches and tell when and why to use them. The demonstration should be planned and carried out without the aid of the teacher, and the speaker's conclusions should be judged understandable, practical, and interesting by nine out of ten pupils.

6. *Communicating Findings and Conclusions.* Students are to take a series of black-and-white photographs of experiments and mount and title them in such a way that they communicate experimental procedures and results in a more effective way than a written report on the same experiment. Effectiveness will be determined by peer evaluation of the two forms of reports.

Practice

On any topic, students should be able to define a problem gather information about the problem, organize and interpret data, develop and test hypotheses, formulate conclusions, and communicate these conclusions to others. Like most scientists, they probably will not apply the six skills in linear fashion. Bearing this in mind, develop a behavioral objective for each skill listed below. Be sure that each objective contains a clear description of the behavior sought, conditions affecting performance, levels of proficiency, and means for judging or testing behavior.

1. *Defining a Problem*
2. *Gathering Information Through Observing, Measuring, Testing, and Experimenting*
3. *Organizing and Interpreting Data*
4. *Generating Hypotheses and Possible Solutions*
5. *Forming Conclusions*
6. *Communicating Findings and Conclusions to Others*

Objectives Concerning Product

Out of his boundless energy man produces inventions, technological processes, and new ways of conceptualizing and of applying knowledge. These products act as an index of a nation's industrial might, standard of living, and sophistication. Examples of objectives emphasizing *product* are:

1. Students are to make inexpensive fire extinguishers capable of putting out small grease or oil fires in a kitchen. Under the supervision of their teacher, they test the effectiveness of the extinguishers in a laboratory or other safe place. The fire extinguishers should completely put out the experimental fires.
2. Students prepare fifty cc of distilled water, made from muddy water through evaporation and condensation, using a flask, rubber or glass tubing, a jar, and a stove or Bunsen burner. The distilled water should appear perfectly clear.
3. Under the supervision of his science teacher, the student prepares ten cc of a gas by using dilute sulphuric acid and zinc. He collects the gas through the displacement of water, and conducts a test that identifies the gas as hydrogen.
4. Students compare the relative importance of the invention of the automobile and the formulation of the formula $E=MC^2$, preparing either a ten-minute oral report or a 500-word written statement. The comparison should include reference to both the constructive and destructive natures of each product.

Objectives Concerning Knowledge

Formed into conceptual systems, the block of knowledge called *science* enables man to comprehend, to manipulate, and to evaluate key elements of the physical and biological world. Through knowledge objectives, teachers can help children learn and understand scientific facts, principles, and theories. These objectives help students acquire a scientific vocabulary; they grow in their knowledge of various ways to structure data, of scientists' behaviors and skills, and of the criteria scientists use to analyze and evaluate phenomena.

Behavioral objectives for acquiring *knowledge* might include:

1. After a study of heat, first-grade pupils make pictures showing that people need a source of heat to keep warm and to prepare certain foods.

2. Second-grade pupils are to learn the functions of five tools used in the home, after a one-week study of the use and care of common tools. Eighty percent of the pupils are to pick up five tools in succession, identify them, tell how they are used, and tell how to take care of them.

3. To learn characteristics of water, second-grade pupils observe what happens to water when it freezes and when it boils; when it is poured into differently shaped containers; when a blotter is dipped into the water; and when water is sprayed on burning matches. Following these observations, five out of seven pupils are able to describe to the class one of the characteristics of water.

4. To show that they have learned the characteristics of types of rocks, fifth-grade pupils are to (a) write definitions of igneous, metamorphic, and sedimentary rocks, and (b) indicate on a matching quiz in which category each of a number of rocks belongs. Nine out of ten pupils are to respond correctly to both parts of this assignment.

5. Fifth-grade pupils are to write 500-word papers on sources of power. When reviewed by the teacher, every paper should include a statement about or description of human and animal muscle power, water power, wind power, electrical power, and nuclear power.

6. To acquire basic concepts about scientific progress through recorded history, ninth-grade students are to read portions of teacher-recommended history textbooks and other material on the history of medicine, engineering, navigation, or communication. Following the reading and study, ninety percent of the students are to score at or above the ninety-fifth percentile on teacher-made tests on the topics.

7. Within a ten-minute period, eleventh-grade chemistry students are to list five inorganic and five organic substances, and to list and describe five acids and five bases. This is to be done after two class periods and a library assignment on organic and inorganic substances, and after two laboratory periods in which the students test ten acids

and ten bases with litmus paper. Eight out of ten students are to complete this assignment without error.

8. Twelfth-grade science students are to demonstrate their knowledge of scientific terminology and of important men of science by (a) listing and defining five technical terms commonly used by meteorologists, nuclear physicists, physicians, astronauts, electronics experts, and mechanical engineers, and (b) matching on a test the names of ten scientists and the fields they represent.

Higher Cognitive Skills

The study of science concerns *knowing,* along a continuum from the simple perception and acquisition of knowledge to the comprehension that results from experience with a set of data or phenomena. Knowledge, comprehension, and skill should be the goals of ob ectives written for this continuum. They may also reflect scientific attitudes, interests, and motivations.

Perhaps at this point it is desirable to recall that, although constructed as a hierarchy, much overlap is evident among the goals, categories, or levels in the "Cognitive Domain" of the *Taxonomy of Educational Objectives.* Because of the cumulative nature of this domain, the skills developed in previous levels are part of each successively higher level. For example, in addition to requiring a particular set of facts, a teacher may see that a synthesis results when these facts are translated, interpreted, extrapolated, and applied. It is also important to recognize that different cognitive levels may be elicited by the same question or statement, because pupils will have had differences in their preliminary learning experiences.

Recognizing the probability of overlap and of such variety in cognitive levels, we can still use the categories of the *Taxonomy* to classify behavioral objectives.

Practice

Using the categories of the *Taxonomy* (knowledge, translation, interpretation, extrapolation, application, analysis, synthesis, and evaluation), determine the level at which each of the following objectives belongs:

1. After watching demonstrations involving mechanical, chemical, and electrical energy, four out of six first-grade pupils answer a question on a verbal science quiz by stating that energy is needed to put an object into motion or to change the direction of a moving object.

2. Following an exercise in which each pupil makes his own magnetic compass from a needle, cork, magnet, and bowl of water, pupils are to judge the accuracy of their home-made compasses by comparing the direction the needle points with the direction of the needle of an accurate laboratory, mariner, or Boy Scout compass.

3. Pupils manipulate seven metal balls suspended by strings from a wooden frame, in three different ways. The principle that for every action there is an equal and opposite reaction should be evident to seventy percent of a sixth-grade science class.

4. Students are to prepare a tape recording which, in the judgment of a high-school physics teacher, contains the same information as four physics formulas chosen by the teacher.

5. After a discussion of the role of scientists in our society, students prepare 500-word statements telling of instances when scientists have spoken out on major political matters. Each statement should mention at least five scientists, five political issues, and five periods of American history.

6. Students formulate criteria for evaluating the roles of scientists in political matters and apply these criteria to judge whether or not the political activities of H-bomb scientists were detrimental to national security.

7. Students view a science-fiction movie, such as *2001: A Space Odyssey,* and determine which aspects of the film they would judge probable within this century. They make a list of at least twenty of these conditions, events, inventions, and discoveries.

8. Students are to study the relationship of plant and animal life in a balanced aquarium and determine the effect on the ecology of the aquarium, first, when fifty percent of the plant life is removed and, second, when fifty percent of the animal life is removed.

9. Three out of five students participate in a science fair by designing projects that receive awards or honorable mentions for being original, worthwhile, and clear in their message and presentation of information.

10. After studying the chemical formulas of common substances, ninety percent of the students write with no errors the chemical formulas for water, cane sugar, and table salt.

11. Using litmus paper, students determine whether a certain unknown liquid is an acid or a base. Their findings should be confirmed by the person who prepared the unknown liquid.

12. Students are to describe in words a chemical reaction. Descriptions should contain the correct words for initial substances, products, and processes.
13. Students determine why certain chemical reactions proceed at a more rapid rate when heat is applied. The students verify their determinations with authoritative reference materials, such as encyclopedias or textbooks.
14. After reading and experimentation, students decide which of the following is the best source of heat for most laboratory experiments: Bunsen burner, alcohol burner, or hot plate.

The cognitive levels intended by the author for the objectives are given on page 121.

Now write at least one behavioral objective in science for each level of the *Taxonomy;* then check to see that your objectives contain the essential characteristics described earlier, and file the objectives in your file box.

Creative Skills

Creativity in science may be an attitude and process for extending awareness of knowledge, processes, and relationships, overcoming obstacles to logical or intuitive thought, and creating original and worthwhile products. Scientists and students of science may reveal their creativity in (1) systematic analysis of change in man and his environment; (2) exploration of causes of phenomena; (3) generation of heuristic attitudes, "if-then" thinking, inductive searches for guiding principles and solutions, and deductive delineations and examinations of the components of natural laws, principles, or generalizations; and (4) construction of conceptions of order and relationships among concepts, principles, and processes.

Creative skills are a means of extending the definition and the focus of science from factual knowledge to ways of knowing. Higher cognitive skills contribute to and are part of this process, for the scientist interprets phenomena from many perspectives, and analyzes and applies data from all available sources when solving a problem or creating a product. The process is reinforced by fluent and flexible thinking, convergent and divergent thought, and sensitivity to problems and relationships.

Fluency in thinking depends to a large extent upon a reservoir of knowledge. Part of a teacher's job is to saturate students' minds with relevant facts. But what is and what is not relevant in the creative process is often difficult to determine, for what may seem trivial may in fact be significant. However, the sheer amount of factual knowledge dictates that teachers attempt to identify which data are significant and which are extraneous.

Sometimes teachers get so involved in systematizing available knowledge that they have little time or energy left to explore new fields of thought. Perhaps teachers can learn to be not only fluent but also flexible in their cerebration, and teach this skill to their pupils. This implies not only generating a vast quantity of ideas and having them flow smoothly into the process of inquiry, but also doing things in new ways, seeing facts in new perspectives, and applying and testing principles and hypotheses in new setting. To some extent this will mean elaborating on what we may already know, adding to or rearranging the facts and principles in a system, or the elements in a physical structure. Flexibility implies getting out of perceptual sets and habitual ways of observing, analyzing, interpreting, manipulating, and relating. At times it leads, beyond elaboration to the creation of an entirely new thought or tangible product.

To do all the things suggested in this section implies discipline—and possibly even the application of certain systems in discovering and creating. Part of a systematized approach may actually involve saturating minds with facts and experience and then allowing the facts and other residue of experience to co-mingle and settle. The term often given to this step of discovery or creation is *incubation*. It is a step that should be planned for and made a part of the student's schedule. Unstructured and free time may contribute to the generation of new ideas and to the resolution of problems.

Following are a few examples of creative skill objectives in science:

1. After learning the general principles of water purification, fifth-grade pupils are to describe at least three basically different ways of purifying water. These methods are to be judged basically different and plausible, or are to be identified as processes currently used to purify water, by a panel of three science teachers. *(Fluency, flexibility, and originality)*

2. Tenth-grade college-preparatory students in biology are to learn the common and scientific names of five birds, five mammals, five reptiles, five fish, and five insects, and to match with no more than one error the common and scientific names of these animals in a five-minute quiz. *(Fluency)*

3. After studying conservation, two out of three third- or fourth-grade students are able to suggest three or more different ways of controlling pollution of the Great Lakes or of San Francisco Bay. The sources of suggestions are to be class discussions, newspaper editorials, and articles in scientific journals. *(Fluency* and *flexibility)*

4. Following a discussion of health and disease, third-grade pupils are to suggest at least three ways of improving their health at home and at school. *(Fluency)*

5. As a result of a fifteen-minute brainstorming session, ten twelfth-grade science students are to generate at least three original ways of forecasting weather, preserving food, traveling in space, or transporting water, gas, or sand. *(Fluency* and *originality)*

6. Students are to develop a series of information-procuring steps by which they can determine whether or not a given substance is poisonous. The steps are to tell how to utilize reference books, resource persons and laboratory tests. *(Elaboration)*

7. Groups of eighth-grade students list different types of substances that dissolve in distilled water at 78° F. This is to be done after studying solutions and the properties of substances that dissolve in water, and after attempting to dissolve various substances in water. Eight different substances are to be listed by each of three separate groups of students. *(Fluency)*

8. Pupils are to identify or formulate designs for at least three different experiments to prove that fish need oxygen to live, that certain air contains pollutants, or that plants need different substances in the soil in order to grow. *(Fluency)*

Craftsmanship Skills

Craftsmanship is generally associated with fashioning products in one of the arts or in a trade. Actually, there is little reason for such a limited definition. Craftsmanship might refer equally well to composing a piece of music, drafting a political or legal document, or composing a sentence, paragraph, short story, poem, or novel. Craftsmanship might include: preparing a reasonable plan, selecting appropriate tools, choosing proper materials, and applying tools skillfully in creating a useful, beautiful, accurate, or worthwhile product.

In the field of science, one can note the need for craftsmanship by the surgeon or biochemist. Craftsmanship is also needed by students and teachers in making and using experimental equipment, hand-crafted models, and diagrams of new machines. It is likewise needed in reconstructing a pottery bowl from a fragment or in building a reflector telescope. Examples of craftsmanship behavioral objectives are:

1. Students draw with pen and India ink a diagram of a nuclear power plant that could provide electrical power for a city of 200,000 persons. All parts of the diagram must be labeled and must be clearly visible from six feet away by persons with normal vision.
2. With plastic, wood, or metal, or any combination of these items, students are to construct a model of a submarine that could be used to recover nodules of manganese at an ocean depth of 200 feet. The model should be at least two feet long and contain movable parts to show how the submarine recovery process would work.
3. Students are to design and build a go-cart capable of carrying a 150-pound person and accelerating from zero to twenty miles per hour in fifteen seconds. The design and go-cart itself will be judged successful if, in eighteen out of twenty time trials, it does accelerate to twenty miles per hour in fifteen seconds or less, and if the frame does not break under the weight of a 150-pound driver.
4. Students arrange correctly the bones of a rabbit or another animal into a skeleton and wire them together or mount them on a board.

Sample Behavioral Objectives — Biology

From ancient Greece to modern time, philosophers have attempted to unify concepts of mind and body and to appreciate the role of each and of both in the human organism. Botanists and zoologists have specialized in solving the puzzling mysteries of plant and animal life. Recently, however, we have begun to emphasize biological processes and systems rather than knowledge about elements and structures. We have begun to think more earnestly about improving not only sweetpeas and pigs, but man.

The field of biology lends itself well to illustration of behavioral objectives in science. A teacher specializing in another scientific area might note these illustrations and apply his knowledge and skill in building a similar file in his own field.

Higher Cognitive Skills

Behavioral objectives for six levels of higher cognitive skills are illustrated in the examples that follow. An attempt has been made to provide a variety of formats and objectives at various grade levels.

Knowledge. To frame an objective at this level, a teacher must ask himself what knowledge in the field of biology he considers worth remembering. Then he can proceed to formulate behavioral objectives such as these:

1. After a two-week period in which the kindergarten child cares for a small plant, he shows by a pictorial or verbal explanation that he recognizes that plants need water and light.
2. Fifth-grade pupils learn three characteristics that distinguish mammals from fish. Following instruction in these characteristics, each pupil demonstrates his knowledge by listing the characteristics in a three-minute quiz.
3. To demonstrate understanding of basic terminology in biology, three out of four students in a high-school biology class write a correct definition for at least twelve of the following terms: *bacillus, conjugation, mutation, anthropomorphism, marsupial, acromegaly, enzyme, protein, nitrogen fixation, monocotyledon, meiosis, chloroplast, cambium, cytoplasm, deoxyribonucleic acid, photosynthesis, hemoglobin, mitochondria, taxonomy, ciliated epithelium.*

Comprehension. Comprehension skills include interpretation, translation, and extrapolation. Interpretation means recognizing and expressing relationships among factual knowledge and among skills and processes. It may also mean rearranging or reordering concepts and principles, and perceiving them from the background of one's accumulated knowledge, understanding, and experience.

The cognitive process of translation involves taking facts, processes, principles, or explanations and communicating them in new ways. In the study of biology, the student should develop the ability to translate scientific terminology into words used in everyday language, and gain facility in explaining an advanced concept to persons not as knowledgeable or sophisticated in science. He should learn to portray on graphs or charts or through chemical or mathematical formulas certain written statements that appear in textbooks or reference books.

Extrapolation is the skill of projecting the effects of certain conditions, behaviors, or procedures. The biologist and the student of biology are involved in extrapolation when they speculate on the possible results of altering ecological settings in which there is a balance among forms of plant and animal life; of altering diets of animals or of the amount of sunlight, water, and nutrients in growing plants; of interrupting the life cycle of certain insects; and of using certain pharmaceuticals to control or eradicate disease.

Following are examples of behavioral objectives involving and fostering comprehension through the skills of interpretation, translation, and extrapolation:

1. After visiting a zoo and a pet shop, seventy-five percent of the children in a kindergarten class tell their teacher the names of three animals that are usually good pets and three animals that are too dangerous to have as pets. All children are to show willingness to avoid contact with the animals that are usually dangerous, as well as freedom from fear of harmless animals. The teacher is to assess a child's understanding of which animals are harmless by holding up pictures of different animals, then asking, "Would you pet this animal? Why, or why not?" *(Interpretation)*

2. Students are to rewrite the following statement in words that an average fifth-grade student can understand: "Sexual reproduction in plants started when spores, probably similar to ulothrix, began behaving as gametes." *(Translation)*

3. Tenth-grade students are to (a) interpret what is meant by the binomial system for naming species; (b) use the system in giving the names of three plants and three animals; (c) translate scientific names for seashells; and (d) create binomial names for three described imaginary plants or animals. *(Interpretation and translation)*

4. Tenth-grade students are to describe in their own words the nitrogen cycle in nature. The description should incorporate the student's point of view regarding the nitrogen cycle, portray the process with formulas and diagrams, and use accurately scientific terms that have been defined during class discussions concerning the cycle. *(Interpretation and translation)*

5. Tenth-grade students are to reword the following statement in the minimum number of words needed to convey the meaning of the statement to nine out of ten classmates: *Like the Sirens who lured Odysseus, the attractive force of the ova emanates over and through the sea. Chemotropism, usually involving weak organic acids, lures the sperm to a*

portion of the oögonium where the final conquest is made. The number of words in the abbreviated statement should be no more than fifty percent of the words in the original statement. *(Translation)*

Application. Application-level thinking may mean applying data, principles, and skills to new situations. It may mean reaching out beyond the confines of particular academic disciplines or career fields for data, principles, and skills to solve a problem. Some behavioral objectives at this cognitive level are:

1. Students in a ninth-grade class or science club are to apply their knowledge of plant nutrition and growth by raising strawberries through hydroponics. Seven out of eight plants used in this experiment are to survive and bear strawberries.
2. First-grade pupils are to use their knowledge of animal needs in caring in their classroom for a turtle, a mouse, a rabbit, a snake, and a parakeet. Pupils are to be divided into teams and are to follow procedures recommended in an authoritative manual on animal care.
3. To demonstrate their proficiency in conducting an experiment and in recording data both in a daily logbook and on charts, fifth-grade pupils are to select one of a number of possible experiments on plant nutrition, growth of molds, or preparation of a balanced aquarium. They then are to conduct experiments, following routines and procedures agreed upon by the class and teacher regarding setting up and conducting an experiment, observing results, recording results, and formulating and presenting research findings. Nine out of ten pupils are to follow agreed-upon routines and procedures and to record data in a manner judged satisfactory by the teacher. Criteria for such a judgment will be developed and agreed upon by pupils and the teacher prior to the experiment.
4. Kindergarten pupils are to develop health habits, such as using a handkerchief, washing hands before eating and after going to the lavatory, and telling the teacher if they feel ill. In doing these things, eighty-five percent of the pupils show that they are applying health habits learned during the first two weeks of school.

Analysis. Analysis consists of breaking down a problem, a body of facts, a behavior, or a description into component elements. The purpose of analysis is to find out what these elements are in order to solve a problem, to achieve a greater understanding, or to accomplish a synthesis of parts or ideas.

Examples of behavioral objectives that involve or foster skills of analysis are:

1. First-grade children are to look carefully for five minutes at a square yard of lawn, a forest floor, or a tidewater pool and then tell the different types of life they see.
2. After observing lichens, algae, and fungi, students are to use their observations and any available reference books to determine the characteristics that distinguish lichens from algae and fungi and to tell what algae and fungi contribute to the life processes of lichens.

Synthesis. When we synthesize, we create something new either by rearranging the parts of some structure or by bringing together thoughts, facts, elements, and ideas from a number of sources to create a new product. Examples of behavioral objectives at the synthesis level are:

1. Tenth-grade biology students are to use a teacher-prepared list of terms correctly in preparing a written description of *selaginella.* Ninety-five percent of the students are to write descriptions judged accurate, clear, and comprehensive by a high-school biology teacher.
2. Using plastic, wooden rods, bands of sheet metal, glue, and paint, students fabricate a model of DNA or starch. Persons familiar with the composition and structure of DNA and starch should recognize the models.

Evaluation. Evaluation is the cognitive level or skill judged to be highest in the hierarchy of objectives in the *Taxonomy.* When we evaluate, we do so on the basis of external standards or criteria, or on the basis of internal criteria or values. Behavioral objectives at this level might include:

1. After reading pertinent articles, twelfth-grade students are to evaluate the following statement: "Contagious sterilization through hormonal insecticides is more desirable and effective as a means of killing insects than either sterilization of males by radiation, or use of DDT." The evaluation is to be made in a written report in which (a) the following terms are defined: *contagious sterilization, hormonal insecticides,* and *radiation;* and (b) criteria are stated and applied for determining what are desirable and effective means of killing insects.
2. Following a study of pollution, seventh-grade students are to rate in descending order of urgency the following reasons for combating pollution of oceans and salt-water bays: (a) to eliminate foul odors and unsightly debris, (b) to prevent commercial loss of shrimp, clams, and fish,

and (c) to stop contamination that adversely affects marine plankton.

3. Students list in descending order of importance the following reasons for studying marine biology: (a) to increase the harvest of fish; (b) to open up new frontiers of knowledge; (c) to acquire knowledge that will enable man to live for long periods of time under the sea; (d) to procure marine plant and animal organisms useful in biomedical research; (e) to uncover knowledge that will enable man to exploit more fully the commercial possibilities of sea life; and (f) to increase the production of plankton.

4. Students are to develop criteria for evaluating locomotion on land, in the water, and in the air. They are to apply these criteria in evaluating the effectiveness of locomotion of (a) measuring worm, caribou, armadillo, cheetah, and man; (b) sea otter, crocodile, and turtle; (c) octopus, salmon, and whale; and (d) golden eagle, hummingbird, and housefly. The evaluations should show in written and diagram form (a) the comparative speeds of different land animals, of different animals that live in the water, of different animals that travel through the air, and of different animals that live both on land and in the water; (b) the comparative speeds of different groups of animals: land animals, animals that live in the water, animals that live on land and in the water, and animals that travel through the air; (c) the comparative speeds of animals with different types of feet; and (d) the comparative ease with which different animals move through or over natural obstacles.

Creative Skills

Creativity, as used to develop these objectives in biology, means developing attitudes, processes, and skills by which man becomes more aware of life in his biosphere and ecosystem, of interrelationships among all forms of life, and of the ways in which plants and animals have adapted to various environmental conditions. It also means an exploration of the paths that teacher and student take to overcome obstacles to understanding elements, structures, functions, and processes of life. At still another level it means creating an original product that has merit in helping us to comprehend ways in which plants and animals live and affect the activities of man. Illustrative of behavioral objectives in this area are these:

1. Pupils "redesign" the human body to make it more adaptable to extremes of hot and cold weather and to life under the sea, more resistant to air and water pollution and to bacteria and viruses, and more resistant to the stress of an

information overload that bombards man through all his waking hours. Each pupil is to suggest at least three changes. Two out of eight suggestions are to be judged highly original by a panel of teachers and students. Before beginning this activity, pupils are to be given criteria that the judges will use and to have studied the structures and functions of amphibians, reptiles, birds, and mammals. *(Originality)*

2. Assuming that the peanut is a perfect food, containing the basic nutrients needed by man, and restricting man's diet to peanuts, milk, coffee, bread, apples, and water, students design a seven-day diet with these substances prepared in many different ways. The diet should not involve the same food substances in the same form during any seventy-two-hour period. *(Originality)*

3. After studying the living habits and habitats of mammals, reptiles, insects, and crustaceans, students design an ideal environment in which men, snakes, tigers, wolverines, large land crabs, and army ants could live together and acquire needed food without harming one another. This design of an environment must show an understanding of the biological and environmental needs of these animals and must be thought to be plausible by sixty percent of the students in the class. *(Originality)*

4. Students list at least five problems that might result from this suggested action: The way to control the population growth of the United States is to eliminate the tax exemption for children and to tax families more for each additional offspring. The rationale for this proposal is that additional children take up living space, use up environmental oxygen, food and community services, and make it more difficult to effect a balance among all forms of life on this planet. Within a ten-minute period, five out of seven students in the seventh-grade should list five problems, judged plausible and basically different by the teacher. *(Sensitivity)*

5. To demonstrate extended awareness of microscopic and macroscopic life, pupils are to describe birds, mammals, bacteria, algae, and other forms of life which they saw for the first time (or distinguishing features they saw for the first time) after instruction in using magnifying glasses, bioscopes, monoculars, and binoculars in studying plant and animal life. Descriptions are to contain information validated by a naturalist, high-school science teacher, or knowledgeable member of the National Audubon Society. *(Awareness)*

6. After a unit on DNA, twelfth-grade students are to write the following statement in at least three different ways: "DNA, a large helical molecule, affects the development of animal life." The three different ways of writing this statement are to contain the same information. That they do will be judged by a high-school science teacher. All students in the class should complete this assignment within twenty minutes. *(Fluency)*

7. Third-grade pupils working in teams of three are to modify an aquarium so that it might be used as a terrarium for salamanders. Three out of four teams are to produce a terrarium in which three salamanders survive for at least a two-month period. *(Flexibility)*

Craftsmanship Skills

Craftsmanship is a skill that can be developed through experiences that are normally a part of biology programs. Examples of behavioral objectives are:

1. Following a study of environments conducive to the health and well-being of small animals, tenth-grade students are to build functional cages which as much as possible duplicate the natural habitat of animals that will live in the cages. By "functional" is meant that the cages can be easily cleaned and moved, and that they are built in such a manner that it is easy to give the animals food and water and remove them from their cages. A majority of the class is to agree that the interiors of seventy percent of the cages do closely resemble the natural habitat, as illustrated by pictures, slides, or films.

2. Fifth-grade students are to use clay and glaze in making replicas of three birds that man uses as food. These replicas are to be one-third life-size and correctly colored (male plumage). The success of this assignment will be judged by having students in other classes identify the replicas. Ninety percent of the responses should be correct.

Discussion Questions and Activities

The following questions and exercises may enable you to assess skills and understandings gained from this chapter in small-group discussions. Leaders of small-group discussions are advised to become thoroughly acquainted with the content of Chapters 1 and 2 and with this chapter, giving particular attention to "Leadership Skills" on page 12. Structure an informal discussion setting that is free from negative judgment of persons and in which each group member assumes responsibility for the professional growth of each other member. Proceed through the questions, allowing enough time for full discussion and for assuring complete understanding. Although much of the information needed to answer the questions may be found in this book, reach outside the confines of these pages to your own background and to the content in suggested readings.

1. Without using any references, create your own definition of science.

2. How does the teaching of science differ from teaching other subject areas? In what ways is it similar?

3. Review the section, "Gauging Pupil Growth and Effectiveness" and then devise a rating sheet for judging degrees of proficiency in the skills and traits identified in this section. Discuss your checklist with fellow teachers and elicit their ideas for refining and testing it with students.

4. In your opinion, what should be the major emphasis of science instruction in kindergarten? Grades one through three? Grades four through six? Grades seven through nine? Grades ten through twelve?

5. What scientific skills might be developed especially in each grade range discussed in question 4?

6. What teaching strategies are particularly effective in helping children acquire concepts, facts, and generalizations?

7. Devise a plan for the deliberate development of each of the processes identified on the AAAS Chart, "Science — A Process Approach."

8. Prepare a concept, cognitive skill, or creative process sequence of five behavioral objectives in science.

Answers to Review Questions
Pages 108–10:

1. Knowledge
2. Evaluation
3. Synthesis
4. Translation
5. Analysis and interpretation
6. Evaluation
7. Extrapolation
8. Synthesis
9. Synthesis
10. Translation
11. Analysis
12. Translation
13. Analysis
14. Evaluation

Bibliography

American Association for the Advancement of Science. "Science—A Process Approach." Chart. New York: Xerox, 1967.

The American Biology Teacher. Washington, D.C.: National Association of Biology Teachers. (All issues.)

Anderson, Ronald D. "Formulating Objectives for Elementary Science, Part I," Science and Children 5, no. 1 (September 1967): 20–23.

Aylesworth, Thomas G. Planning for Effective Science Teaching. Middletown, Conn.: Wesleyan Univ. Press, 1963.

Baker, Jeffrey J. W. In the Beginning: A Survey of Modern Embryology. Columbus, Ohio: American Education Publications, 1964.

Blanc, Sam S. "Creative Thinking for the Process Skills," Science and Children 4, no. 8: 6–7.

Brandwein, Paul F. Substance, Structure, and Style in the Teaching of Science. New York: Harcourt, Brace & World, 1965.

California Association of County Superintendents of Schools. "Implementing the Science Program in California." In Science Resource Guide, Series 5. Donald Lundstrom, ed. Oakland: Alameda County School Department, 1968.

California State Advisory Committee on Science Education. Science Framework for California Public Schools. Sacramento: California State Department of Education, 1970.

Chiapetta, Jerry. "Great Lakes—Great Mess," Audubon 70, no. 3 (May–June 1968): 30–44.

Chimento, Russell L., and Irish, Elmo L. Introduction to Computation in Science—Teacher's Guide. Sacramento, California: Sacramento Unified School District, 1968.

Clark County School District. Interim Curriculum Guide: Science, Level K–12. Las Vegas: Clark County School District, 1969.

Costa, Arthur. "A Passion for Certainty, A Need for Doubt, A Search for Structure." Paper read to the California State Science Framework Committee, Sacramento, 1966.

Drummond, Ainslie, ed. A Basis for Creative Science Teaching. Middletown, Conn.: American Education Publications, 1966.

Education Research Council of America. Life Science Program.

"Effective Use of the Sea." Report of the Panel of Oceanography of the President's Science Advisory Committee. Washington: U.S. Government Printing Office, June 1966.

Gilliam, H. "Praise the Buck and Pass the Dirt," Audubon 70, no. 2 (March–April 1968): 45–8.

Graham, Frank, Jr. "The Breath of Death," Audubon 70, no. 4 (July–August 1968): 49–58.

Haffner, Rudolph E. Genetics—The Thread of Life: New Biology for Young Students. Columbus, Ohio: American Education Publications, 1964.

Haffner, Rudolph E., and Baker, Jeffrey J. W. *The Vital Wheel — Metabolism: An Introduction to Some Biological Chemistry.* Columbus, Ohio: American Education Publications, 1964.

Hallman, Ralph J. "The Necessary and Sufficient Conditions of Creativity," *Creativity: Its Educational Implications.* Edited by John Curtis Gowan, George D. Demos, and E. Paul Torrance. New York: John Wiley & Sons, 1967.

Lessing, Lawrence. "A Molecular Bomb for the War Against Insects," *Fortune 77*, no. 1 (July 1968): 87–9, 116, 118, 121.

MacLean, Donald A., and Hinton, Sam. *The Sea: A New Frontier.* Pasadena, California: Franklin Publications, 1967.

McAnally, John S. *Chemistry.* Columbus, Ohio: Charles E. Merrill, 1966.

Newsletter. Washington: American Association for the Advancement of Science. (All issues.)

Osborne, Alex F. *Applied Imagination.* New York: Scribner's, 1957.

Science. Washington: American Association for the Advancement of Science. (All issues.)

Science and Children. Washington: National Science Teachers Association. (All issues.)

Science Curriculum Improvement Study. *SCIS Newsletter.* Berkeley, Calif.: Regents of the University of California. (All issues.)

The Science Teacher. Washington: National Science Teachers Association. (All issues.)

Stendler, Celia. *The Developmental Approach of Piaget and Its Implications for Science in the Elementary Schools.* New York: Macmillan, 1966.

Suchman, J. Richard. *Developing Inquiry in Earth Science.* Chicago: Science Research Associates, 1968.

UNESCO. *UNESCO Source Book for Science Teaching.* New York: UNESCO, 1956.

Wallas, Graham. *The Art of Thought.* New York: Harcourt, Brace, 1926.

CHAPTER 7

READING

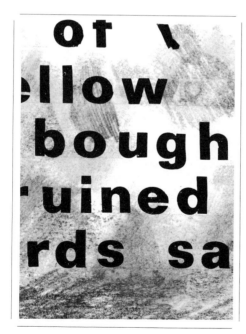

7

Rationale and Methods

Gauging Pupil Growth and Effectiveness

Academic Skills

Higher Cognitive Skills

Creative Skills

From the world around him, man selectively perceives certain objects and symbols. These he invests with meaning, highly personal and unique to him. This is true whether the object or symbol is a new car, a mathematical equation, a stop sign, or the printed word.

Bombarded with a host of auditory and visual stimuli, the child learns to pull to the fore perceptually the black marks from a black and white page. This he does as he invests them with meaning and sound. This he does in competition with pictures that tell a story, lights, colors, nearby persons, fascinating objects at home and at school, and his memory.

Reading is an attending, receiving, mediating process in which visual stimuli attract attention, are directed to the brain, and are interpreted in light of past experience. Reading is more than seeing and more than attaching accepted definitions to words. We bring ourselves to each word, group of words, or stimulus. To each we bring our background, comprehension, and perception of meaning. Through reading we can define the parameters of our being and discover who we are. Reading is a means of learning how the person we perceive ourselves to be fits into the total scheme of things — into a world, a nation, a number of communities, a household, an extended family, and a number of groups and organizations.

Within the total milieu of language, reading plays an important part as one of the language arts; other language arts skills, such as listening and speaking, precede it. An effective teacher of reading must recognize and use to advantage the interrelationships that exist among these skills.

Rationale and Methods

Teaching manuals and curriculum guides list numerous general and specific objectives to be pursued in a reading program. Without referring specifically to any of these, perhaps we can say that a child is taught to read in order that he might know himself and his world; test his own ideas and experiences vicariously with those of many authors; become proficient in abstract, critical, logical, expressive, and descriptive thought; and order his world with categories, labels, and systems of ideas. Reading is the gateway to success in most areas of the school curriculum and to achievement in most professional and technical careers. It is also a means of stimulating interests and of achieving pleasure.

How Reading Is Taught

Teachers and reading specialists find it necessary to assess a child's background and to approach the teaching of reading by presenting to a child a range of experiences. Careful attention is given to a child's physical and intellectual development, emotional and psychological stance, and environmental stimuli. Teachers and reading specialists make judgments about and attempt to improve a child's visual discrimination, visual perception, form constancy, coherence of thought, and interest in reading, using in the process many different methods of teaching these skills.

The debate over methods of teaching reading skills has raged for years, being modified now and then by some new or refurbished method.[1] Advocates and opponents of certain methods often find themselves in a position of stalemate — not altogether a surprise when the name of the game is "doing what is best for the individual." Each child has his own unique traits that affect competence in reading. Some children seem to learn best through auditory stimulation, others through visual stimulation, and still others through kinesthetic means. Because children probably remember more of what they see than of what they hear, an experience involving both sight and sound is likely to be remembered longer than an experience involving only one of the senses.

The purpose of this chapter is not to enter the great debate but rather to help teachers acquire skill in preparing behavioral objectives in the area of reading. Before doing this, however, it is appropriate to consider how a child learns to read, ways of teaching reading, and techniques for gauging pupil growth and effectiveness in reading.

Responding to perceived patterns of speech, a child develops his own tentative rules, principles, and rationale for language structure and usage. For example, having mastered the verb *go*, he may then proceed to *goed* to express the past tense. Hypothesizing constantly, a child builds his own set of guidelines for attacking and mastering an enormous array of thoughts expressed in words, sentences, and paragraphs.

1. See Jeanne Chall, *Learning to Read — The Great Debate* (New York: McGraw-Hill, 1967).

In doing this he makes certain sound-word associations which begin to pyramid, interrelate, and correlate as he progresses through language experiences at home and at school. Before proceeding very far along this path, and often as an initial school experience, he will learn the alphabet as a means of discriminating between different letters and sounds. He must learn to distinguish between similar letters (such as *b* and *d*, *c* and *s*, and *t* and *l*) and to associate certain sounds with words or portions of words. These auditory and visual skills are antecedent to learning to read: a child should first be given associative experiences that are controlled or programmed, and his school experience should foster his perceptual, conceptual, and skill development. He then progresses rapidly to language understanding, word mastery, and the independent decoding of unfamiliar words, written sequences of thought, and the structure of his language. Along the way, he encounters words that do not fit his own rules or the regular patterns or rules with which he is familiar. These he learns to master as part of his sight vocabulary.

In practice, aspects of various methods, including those following, may be incorporated into a program for the benefit of different children at different stages. Ideally, a teacher's approach is diagnostic and eclectic: instructions, treatments, and prescriptions are directed toward meeting pupils' decoding, communicating, and ordering needs.

Linguistic Method

There are a number of variations of what has been called the linguistic method, all of which seem to stress a child's own associations of printed words with the sounds and sound patterns of his speech. Through a constant testing and refining process, a child develops his own rationale and rules for sound-letter association and spelling. These he applies automatically and almost unconsciously in his reading.

Language-Experience Method

In this method, the teacher develops reading skills through a child's own experiences with objects and words. A child dictates his own stories and sees his spoken words translated into written words. As a result, he perceives reading as "talk written down." Gradually a child learns how to substitute written symbols and patterns for auditory speech. This approach has been found to be especially effective during the early stages of learning to read, and it may be a valuable adjunct to other methods. One of the problems encountered in the use of this method is that a child tends to memorize rather than to read the materials. Another problem is the lack of a controlled vocabulary.

Sight and "Look-Say" Method

Through experiences in association, a word, phrase, or sentence becomes for a child the stimulus for an oral response. The meaning developed through or inherent in the oral response is transferred to the written symbol and, in time, a child learns how to read through associating a symbol with its meaning without going through the intermediate step of subvocalizing. Problems associated with the sight and look-say method include the possibilities of making reversals, such as seeing *was* and saying *saw*, and of confusing words that look alike, such as *house* and *horse*.

Phonetic and Structural Analysis Methods

The essential elements of the phonetic method of teaching reading are letter sounds, blends of various letters, and sound-meaning units in words. Words are analyzed into phonograms, so that the reading processes involve units and patterns of sound rather than letters. Other aspects of the phonetic method are writing sound patterns and words and memorizing rules. There are hazards involved in relying upon phonetic rules, however, since in some situations they may apply only forty-five to sixty percent of the time. The emphasis upon drill rather than upon meaning loses the interest of many children. The method may also lead to word-by-word reading and diminished fluency. In spite of the possible pitfalls, this method has efficacy, and some children seem to learn best by it.

Structural analysis, like the phonetic method, involves learning to read by assessing key elements of words. Whereas the phonetic method emphasizes blending elements of sounds, structural analysis is more concerned with parts of the printed word. Syllables and syllabication, prefixes and suffixes, and words within words become points of word-attack and of comprehension building.

Kinesthetic Method

Tracing letters and words may help children with perceptual-visual handicaps, who confuse similar-looking letters, and those children who need help in acquiring a left-to-right orientation to reading and writing. The sense of touch may be profitably used as a reinforcing sense for certain children who do not make normal progress in the regular reading program.

Individualized-Reading Method

Individualized reading involves the child in his own progression of skill development and concept formation. One type of individualized reading starts with self-selection of books that a child reads at an independent reading level. These books are ones that will aid him in developing reading skills, allow him to locate information, or satisfy his own desire for recreation. Teacher-pupil conferences provide opportunities for pupil guidance and direction as well as for assessment of his skills. Emphasis in this method is upon skillful use of a wide range of trade books. Grouping of children is done to develop special skills and to aid children with special reading needs and interests. This method of teaching reading requires a well-organized teacher who is skilled in diagnosis and prescription.

A variation of individualized reading is "Individually Prescribed Instruction" (I.P.I.). Currently being field-tested and demonstrated throughout the United States, the system involves clear formulation of behavioral objectives and the following steps for the teacher:

1. Choose instructional objectives stated in behavioral terms.
2. Assess student proficiency or lack of proficiency in the behaviors specified.
3. Prepare a plan, a prescription for overcoming deficiencies and for acquiring competence.
4. Carry out the plan.
5. Evaluate the student's progress continually.
6. Test for mastery of the objectives.[2]

Multimedia and Audiovisual Method

Through creative use of sound and visual images, children can be programmed through a series of basic and reinforcing learning experiences. Transparency overlays, tape recordings, films, film loops, sound-filmstrips, phonograph records, charts, and study prints have many uses. They can prepare a child for initial reading experiences; they introduce sound-symbol association; they foster auditory and visual discrimination; they can build word-attack skills; they can motivate children to engage in a wider range of reading; and they are valuable in building speed and comprehension. Some publishers and teachers are beginning to see the possibilities of greater reinforcement, and possibly greater teaching success, through increased use of audio, visual, and audiovisual materials. These materials can be incorporated successfully into almost all other methods of reading instruction.

Basal-Reader Method

During the past few years, basal readers and supplementary materials have improved considerably. Preprimers, primers,

---

2. Research for Better Schools, Inc., "Teaching in I.P.I. Mathematics" (A Program of Teacher Preparation), Vol. 1 of 6 (Philadelphia: Research for Better Schools, Inc., 1700 Market Street, 1969), p. 44.

readers, workbooks, word-recognition cards, phrase cards, teachers' manuals, and other materials are designed to provide a sequential and developmental program.

As they appear in basal readers, established sequences for motivation and skill development may generally be defensible. However, the job of articulating concept and skill development involves articulating sequences within the individual. The basal reader does give a sense of program-wide continuity, though at times it may be spurious. It may be especially helpful to the inexperienced teacher. According to two authorities in the field, one important change needed in such readers is a shift from the early reliance upon the "look-say" and "meaning" approaches to a decoding (sound-symbol association) approach.[3]

Multiple-Approach Method

A high degree of professional skill may be required when the teacher plans to use a combination of several reading methods. He will need to be expert in diagnosing and prescribing, in order to form an approach that encompasses decoding, comprehension-building, and individual motivation. To do this, he must have some knowledge of how children learn, the problems they encounter in reading a language, effective teaching techniques, and useful and appropriate materials. In using this knowledge, he must call upon his skill in encouraging all aspects of children's skill development — cognitive, affective, and psychomotor.

Teachers nowadays recognize the fallacy of adhering to a single method only. They are aware of the value of multiple approaches, using methods that are best for each child. There is growing awareness of developmental psychology; developmental sequences are recognized as effective that start the learning process with concrete objects and symbols as well as a child's own experience and speech capability. The information that is needed to reinforce the developmental approach is that which describes a child's past experiences, his emotional and social development, his current appraisal of himself, others, and the school setting, and his current skills and abilities. A high degree of creativity is exhibited by the teacher who each day adjusts the classroom learning environment, experiences, and assignments to the perceptual, conceptual, creative, and higher cognitive needs of the individual pupils.

---

3. See Jeanne Chall, "Beginning Reading: Where Do We Go from Here?" *Today's Education* 58 (1969): 37; and Ruth Strang, *Reading*, "Dimensions in Early Learning Series" (San Rafael, Calif.: Dimensions Publishing, 1968), p. 27.

This brief description of methods for teaching reading is intended as general background information. For comprehensive and authoritative reviews of the strengths, weaknesses, and appropriateness of particular methods, the reader may want to consult these sources (listed in the bibliography): DeBoer and Dallman, *The Teaching of Reading;* Gray, *On Their Own in Reading;* Harris, *How To Increase Reading Ability;* Heilman, *Principles and Practices of Teaching Reading;* Spache, *Reading in the Elementary School;* Strang, *Reading;* and Veatch, *Reading in the Elementary School.*

Suggestions for Helping the Child to Read

Although experts differ on methods to use in teaching reading, the following steps might prove helpful:

1. Provide language experiences for the child in an atmosphere of emotional security.
2. Associate aspects of language experience with visual symbols.
3. Translate the child's spoken sentences into written sentences.
4. Develop the child's facility in transforming speech to written symbols and in associating sound and speech patterns with words and parts of words.
5. Build the child's basic sight vocabulary to be used later in formulating sentences.
6. Develop the child's facility in word-attack skills, including structural and phonetic elements.
7. After initial emphasis on decoding, foster the child's literal comprehension and then higher levels of thought and meaning. Recognize the decoding process as an initial step in the continuum of searching for meaning.
8. Adjust the method(s) of teaching reading to the learning style and specific needs of the child. Do not attempt to follow just one approach.
9. Continue to build all identified skills as the child develops, matures, and becomes physically, cognitively, and emotionally ready for more advanced performance in each of these skills.
10. Define the reading task for the child as:
    a. Learning about his natural and social environments and about his relationships to various aspects of these environments;
    b. Increasing his self-understanding;
    c. Developing and refining his interests and skills of thinking; and
    d. Attaining for himself pleasure and joy.

Gauging Pupil Growth and Effectiveness

To judge pupil growth and effectiveness, the teacher refers specifically to measurable skills, content acquisition, and attitude formation in asking questions such as the following:

1. Is the child ready to learn to read?
2. In what ways is he reading better now than he did one month ago, three months ago, or a year ago?
3. Has he shown any noticeable change in speed, comprehension, word-attack skills, and vocabulary and reading level?
4. Has he progressed to an independent reading level that is more mature?
5. Does he have trouble with more than five out of one hundred consecutive words in a basal reader?
6. Has he acquired techniques for (a) gaining meaning from the content, (b) locating information through skimming, scanning, and using library reference skills, and (c) improving speed and comprehension?
7. Does he adjust his rate and style of reading to the nature of the reading material and to his specific purposes for reading the material?

Some of the above questions may be answered through formal and informal reading tests. Answers to other questions might best be obtained through the use of rating scales and other observational checklists and profiles. Determining reading ability and performance usually involves assessing the pupil's skills in reading readiness, basic reading skills, knowledge of sources, and reading traits and attitudes, as listed below.

Reading Readiness Skills

1. Visual perception and discrimination
2. Auditory perception and discrimination
3. Visual memory
4. Eye-hand and general motor coordination
5. Left-right orientation
6. Clear speech involving whole sentences
7. Adequate experiential background
8. Sufficient physical, social, and intellectual maturity
9. Interest in reading
10. Adequate self-concept
11. Attention to and response to reading-readiness activities
12. Ability to work independently

13. Knowledge of word meaning, including an adequate vocabulary
14. Logical and sequential expression of ideas

Basic Skills of Reading

1. Knowledge of the names and sounds of letters of the alphabet
2. Possession of a basic sight vocabulary
3. Ability to analyze and comprehend words
   a. Skill in decoding
      (1) linguistic "pattern" analysis and association of sounds and words
      (2) phonetic and structural analysis
   b. Skill in encoding, or spelling
4. Ability to translate spoken sentences into written speech
5. Fluency
   a. Reading rate (words per minute)
   b. Effective reading rate (words per minute multiplied by percentage or comprehension)
   c. Rate adjusted to purpose of reading and to the nature of the materials
   d. Skimming
   e. Correct eye movement
6. Comprehension
   a. Facts
   b. Main ideas
   c. Literal meaning
   d. Inference
   e. Mood or tone
   f. Accent and other clues indicated by punctuation
7. Extensive reading
   a. Different content fields
   b. Different literary forms
   c. Different literary styles
   d. Different authors
8. Intensive reading
   a. Problem-solving
   b. Acquisition of mastery of a subject area or a portion of a subject area
9. Ability to distinguish among different types of reading material and literary forms.

Knowledge in Reading

1. Ability to use sources of help in:
   a. Word attack

    b. Vocabulary development
       (1) Dictionaries
       (2) Thesauruses
       (3) Glossaries
       (4) Books on the origin of words, word usage, and the changing nature of language
       (5) Reading laboratories
    c. Building comprehension
    d. Improving fluency, including effective reading rate
    e. Development of other reading skills
  2. Utilization of books and children's magazines
  3. Ability to use sources in developing skills of listening, speaking, and writing

Attitudes and Traits in Reading

1. Interest
2. Attention
    a. Awareness
    b. Purposeful reading
3. Responsiveness
    a. To authors' thoughts
    b. To ideas
    c. To facts
    d. To use of words
    e. To tone and mood
4. Concentration
    a. Perception
    b. Discrimination
    c. Inference
    d. Analysis
    e. Evaluation
5. Ease with books and authors
6. Enjoyment
7. Creative responsiveness
8. Openness
    a. To new books and new topics
    b. To new ideas
    c. To new ways of improving skills and enjoyment of reading

Habits in Reading

1. Ability to decode
2. Competence in looking up new words
3. Effectiveness in building word power
4. Comprehension of what is read

5. Consistency in seeking help when at a frustration level of reading
6. Regularity in recreational reading
7. Ability to scan for facts and main ideas
8. Consistency in attempts to improve effective reading rate
9. Choice of different types of reading material

Academic Skills

Some persons would say that it is questionable to term reading an academic subject area, rather than simply a skill to be learned. To some it seems more of a craft than a discipline or branch of knowledge. Yet when it comes to framing behavioral objectives for the teaching of reading, the theoretical argument seems unimportant. What is important is that much time is devoted to the teaching of reading in the elementary school; therefore, behavioral objectives need to be devised to guide the instruction. For convenience, we have grouped some objectives as "academic skills," and others as "higher-cognitive skills." Academic skills include such areas as reading readiness, some basic skills, acquisition of knowledge, attitudes and responses to reading, and reading habits.

Reading Readiness

1. Following a series of games in which he identifies like and unlike objects, the pupil tells with no more than one error which letter in each of nine groups of five letters is different from the rest: *(Visual discrimination)*
   a) a, a, a, o, a
   b) o, o, e, o, o
   c) q, q, q, q, p
   d) m, n, m, m, m
   e) l, l, t, l, l
   f) d, d, d, b, d
   g) w, v, w, w, w
   h) c, c, e, c, c
   i) a, a, a, a, e
2. Listening to a tape recording, a kindergarten pupil is to be able to distinguish with no more than two errors whether the words in twelve similar-sounding pairs are the same or different.
   The list might be:
   hat and *hat*   *ant* and *ant*
   cat and *rat*   *dog* and *doll*

ball and *fall*   *boy* and *girl*
run and *fun*   *tub* and *tub*
tick and *trick*   *cow* and *car*
toy and *boy*   *candy* and *money*
(Auditory discrimination)

3. After the teacher has drawn a simple geometric figure on the chalkboard and covered it up, a kindergarten or first-grade pupil draws the same form. *(Visual memory)*

4. Following games and other experiences in which he counts from left to right, looks at pictures from left to right, and observes three-dimensional objects from left to right, the pupil displays this orientation to the satisfaction of the teacher. The teacher uses a game, such as one in which a pupil thinks of a toy, and other children guess whether it is the first, second, third, or fourth item in a row of pictures. *(Left-to-right orientation)*

5. In a "share-and-tell" period, the first-grade pupil is to speak coherently in complete sentences and describe a series of events in proper sequence. *(Logical and sequential expression of ideas)*

6. Responding to a series of three directions, the pupil performs three tasks in the order requested. These he completes without error in a period of six minutes. *(Listening skill, auditory memory)*

7. Following orientation to audiometric and vision testing, the pupil is to perform on such tests at levels established as satisfactory by a committee of physicians and educators. *(Physical, social, and intellectual maturity)*

Basic Skills of Reading

1. Given a set of fifteen pictures, the pupil arranges the pictures into five rhyming groups without error. *(Auditory discrimination)*

2. Following periods of listening to and saying words from the same word family (e.g., *hat, cat,* and *bat*), the pupil applies his sound-word associations correctly to other words in that word family (e.g., *rat, sat,* and *fat*). *(Auditory discrimination)*

3. To demonstrate adequate word recognition and vocabulary, the pupil is to show that he recognizes on sight all words in his preprimer. The teacher makes this assessment by having the pupil read a list of these words. *(Word recognition)*

4. When the teacher pronounces a word containing a consonant blend, the pupil holds up the card containing the consonant blend, or writes the blend on an individual chalkboard. *(Phonetic analysis)*

5. The pupil is to pronounce correctly eight out of ten unfamiliar words by applying his knowledge of the sounds
of studied phonograms, such as *ight, and, old, ake,* and
ill. (Phonetic analysis)
6. The pupil listens to the teacher say words containing
diagraphs, such as *shield, wheel, child,* and *thunder,* and
stands when he hears words that have a particular initial
diagraph, such as the *ch* in *child.* He also demonstrates
his knowledge of the particular final diagraph sounds for
ch and *sh* by correctly pronouncing *much, such, fish,
dish,* and *wish. (Phonetic analysis)*
7. When confronted with unfamiliar words of a controlled
vocabulary, the pupil demonstrates phonetic and structural analysis in attempting to decipher the meaning and
pronunciation of the words. *(Word-attack skills)*
8. To improve ability to figure out the meaning of new
words, each student in a ninth-grade advanced English
class is to learn the meaning of each of the following
prefixes: *mis-, dis-, poly-, ambu-, alter-, avi-, bene-,
aqua-, dura-, facil-, ego-, mut-, trans-,* and *un-.* Each
student is to demonstrate his understanding of the prefixes by (a) writing definitions for each of them, and
(b) figuring out the meaning of fourteen words made up of
the prefixes attached to known root words. Every student
in the class is to submit at least twelve correct definitions
and be correct in the meanings ascribed to the new
words. *(Structural analysis)*
9. With the help of the teacher and after using reading
laboratory materials a minimum of fifty minutes per
school day for six weeks, high school students with
Stanford-Binet IQs of 130 or higher are to improve their
effective reading rate by 300 percent. *(Comprehension
and fluency)*
10. After reading an adventure classic, the pupil tells how the
setting contributes to the theme. *(Comprehension)*
11. After reading three ten- to twenty-line poems selected by
the teacher, the high-school or college student is to
classify the poems by categories established by the
teacher and the class and also to indicate the mood which
the poets apparently attempted to create and, in fact, did
create in sixty to seventy percent of the students in the
class. *(Comprehension of the tone or mood)*

Knowledge in Reading
1. Confronted with unfamiliar scientific terms, the student
demonstrates his knowledge of reference sources by first
looking in a textbook glossary, and then by consulting

both an abridged and an unabridged dictionary, an encyclopedia, or a scientific dictionary in the specific field. The teacher observes the student use the glossary and one of the other sources.

2. A seventh-grade student, in an "Individually Prescribed Instruction" program or using a multilevel SRA *Reading Laboratory®*, demonstrates his knowledge of the procedure involved by explaining the system to another student. A panel of three students is to judge the explanation satisfactory with respect to its clarity and comprehensiveness.

3. Using a thesaurus, eighth-grade students are to find three or more synonyms for each of ten words selected by the teacher. The assignment is to be completed within thirty minutes and with no more than three errors or omissions.

4. Following an orientation on how to find and select books at their reading levels, fourth-, fifth-, and sixth-grade pupils are to select three books at their own independent reading level from a set of classroom books, the school library, or the public library. To demonstrate that one of the three selections is at an independent rather than at an instructional or frustration reading level, pupils are to read one page to a classmate. Seven out of ten pupils should do this smoothly, with full comprehension, and without having to look up more than one word.

5. To demonstrate knowledge of his reading development to date and of steps he plans to take to improve his reading rate, comprehension, word-attack ability, and pleasure, each high-school student is to develop, with the help of the teacher, a profile of his current attainment in reading skills and a five-step plan for improving his reading during a two-month period.

Attitudes Toward and Responses to Reading

1. Given an opportunity to react to a story or poem read by the teacher, a fifth-grade pupil shows that he is interested and is responding creatively to what was read. He indicates this by expressing divergent thoughts, by making a number of associations between what was read and his own experiences and thoughts, by writing a poem, or by illustrating in two- or three-dimensional art work the major plot or ideas expressed in the story or poem.

2. As a result of orientation in the different purposes for reading materials, each pupil in a fifth-grade English class is to be attentive and concentrate on rate- and comprehension-building tasks during skill-building sessions.

3. As a result of preparatory motivational statements and questions posed by the teacher, the student indicates his eagerness to read a particular book. This is to be evident to classroom visitors by the student's quickly procuring a copy of the story selected, beginning to read it immediately, and apparently being so absorbed in the reading that he neither looks about the room nor appears to be bothered by the presence of visitors.

4. Following instruction and practice in preparing book reviews, students in a ninth-grade English class are to show an objective and critical attitude in analyzing and reporting on the books they read. A panel of students and teachers are to note that these students apply certain established standards and criteria and that they refrain from highly subjective comments and the use of nebulous terminology in describing the books.

5. Each child in a first or second grade is to listen to a tape recording of a humorous story. Then he is to try to read the book. After he has become somewhat familiar with the book, the teacher is to read it aloud. During the reading, each child is to indicate by some response, such as chiming in on repetitive phrases or laughing, that he enjoys the book.

Habits of Reading

It is difficult to draw a line of demarcation between this section and the previous one, for certainly readers do develop habitual ways of perceiving and responding. Although such perceptual sets may at times be too restricting they may also predispose us to desirable activity, affective response, and effective action. The reading process can be facilitated by developed habits of attention, concentration, mental manipulation of ideas, receptivity, analysis and evaluation. The habits highlighted in this section, however, are those that are more specifically related to particular skills. Examples of behavioral objectives are:

1. As a result of instruction and experience in sounding out words, syllables, phonograms, diagraphs, blends, vowels, consonants, and diphthongs, the pupil applies his own linguistic or phonetic rules in pronouncing new words. Competency in such application is to be recognized by a rating of "satisfactory" or "excellent" by the teacher.

2. Students are to read a novel and study teacher-prepared lists of the more difficult words in it. While reading a second novel, and without direction from the teacher, each student is to keep track of new words, look them up in a dictionary, and keep a written record of their definitions.

3. When asked to locate certain facts or main ideas in an article, the pupil demonstrates rapid and efficient scanning techniques. He should show that he adjusts his reading technique, including rate, to the assigned task. This should be done in such a manner as to warrant a rating of "satisfactory" or better.
4. When a word is unfamiliar, the student attempts first to discover its meaning from the reading context. Then he uses other techniques and sources for finding the meaning.
5. By the time a student is in the tenth grade, he should demonstrate that he uses knowledge of prefixes, suffixes, and root words in figuring out the meaning of new words. The teacher should observe this behavior as the student attempts to figure out the meaning of eight unfamiliar words.

Higher Cognitive Skills

Perceptual acuity, intelligence, and creativity are mutually reinforcing factors in the process of learning to read. Higher mental processes and skills are involved in the speed with which auditory and visual stimuli are mediated within the brain, the qualitative aspects of this mediation, the association of words and sounds, the hypothesizing of relationships, and the building of a personal set of word-attack and communication rules.

Although it is typical for eighty-five percent of teaching time to be spent at the lowest of the intellectual levels (knowledge or cognition-memory), teachers should increase their professional competence and satisfaction by teaching at the higher levels — thinking, reacting, solving, and creating. Listed below are behavioral objectives in reading that help to advance the higher cognitive skills outlined in the *Taxonomy*.

Interpretation

1. Each fifth-grade pupil reads three selections of literature assigned by the teacher and determines the authors' purposes in writing the selections. The determination of purpose for two of the selections is to agree with the author's own stated purpose, noted in an authoritative reference.
2. After the teacher has read a story to a first-grade class, each pupil tells whether he thinks the mood conveyed was happy, funny, serious, or sad. Each pupil is to respond in a

manner that the teacher considers appropriate for that individual.

3. As part of an assignment in reading about the background of the Civil War, eleventh-grade students are to prepare a 500-word statement containing their assessment of the major cause or causes, and to indicate whether the authors of books they have read tended to emphasize economic, political, social, or other reasons.

Translation

1. Upon hearing the teacher pronounce words representing patterns learned and upon seeing the teacher point to objects brought into the classroom for this experience, second-grade pupils are to change the teacher's spoken words into printed words on a piece of paper or chalkboard, or are to arrange tagboard letters into appropriate words.

2. After reading the same basic content in both a technical and in a recreational-reading form, students in an eighth-grade class read six other selections furnished by the teacher and indicate correctly which selections are examples of technical reading and which are examples of recreational reading.

3. Pupils are to rewrite in traditional orthography and with no errors three sentences originally printed in the initial teaching alphabet (i/t/a).

Extrapolation

1. After assessing the literal meaning of a piece of writing, and the inferences of the author, the student is to extend some of the author's thoughts and ideas beyond those understood or inferred. Each student is to do this in not more than three paragraphs.

2. Having read several short stories by the same author, the student writes a short story of his own, using the same style as the author. This he does in such a way that fifty percent of the students identify the student's short story with the style of the author he is imitating.

3. Following the teacher's reading of most of a story, the pupil relates how he thinks the story might end. Responses should be judged by the teacher as a plausible and logical extension of facts and incidents that have been read.

Application

1. Having formulated his own rules for pronunciation of monosyllabic words in which a vowel is surrounded by

consonants, the pupil is to apply his rule to six other mono-syllabic words. This should be done in a manner judged logical by the teacher.

2. Using knowledge of root words, prefixes, and suffixes, ninth-grade students demonstrate to their English teacher their ability to figure out the meaning of sixty percent of the words on a list prepared by the teacher.

3. Recalling the basic elements of music (harmony, melody, rhythm, tone color, and form), students are to create an analogy between this set of elements and the basic elements of oral reading. Each analogy is to be judged reasonable by a panel of two students and the teacher.

4. To the satisfaction of the teacher, pupils are to apply phonetic understandings in determining whether the c's in the following words have a soft or a hard c sound: call, celler, Chicago, car, cornice, and circle.

5. Having developed a basic sight vocabulary, the pupil, while in a reading group, is to be able to recognize these sight words instantly when they are included on an experience chart or in a primer. This assessment is to be made by the teacher.

Analysis

1. In looking at the following words, sixty percent of the pupils are to say with no more than two errors how the words in each pair look the same and how they look different: ball and doll, cat and rat, milk and silk, fun and sun, rug and hug. Pupils are also to state how the words sound the same and how they sound different.

2. Eighth-grade students are to study stories by a particular author and then tell how that author used certain words to create a particular response, such as a feeling of happiness, apprehension, or commitment to act on the part of the reader.

3. Fifth-grade students are to list three words or phrases that tend to evoke each of the following feelings: joy, solemnity, anger, patriotism, and abhorrence. Each student's listing of words should be agreed to by seventy percent of the class.

4. After listening to or reading a short story, the pupil lists in proper sequence three or more events in the story.

5. Children judged to be ready for reading correctly select the two rhyming pictures from a group of three in each of five sets.

6. After looking at a mixed-up sequence of four pictures of an activity, the pupil is to arrange them in logical sequence.

Synthesis

1. Pupils involved in a linguistic approach to learning to read are to record in a notebook their insights into word-sound relationships and rules that they tentatively form in attacking new words. Over a period of time designated by the teacher, each child's observations are to be formulated into a design or set of rules. Each set of observations can be compared with standard phonetic rules, and evaluated in terms of its effectiveness as a guide to the child's actions. A team composed of a teacher, a school psychologist, and a reading specialist is to judge the design adequate for the individual.

2. Pupils learning to read by a phonetic method are to formulate a written plan for determining when to apply certain rules and are to show little or no evidence of anxiety if there are exceptions to those rules forty-five to sixty percent of the time.

3. Following a study of different approaches to learning to read, students in a high-school Future Teachers of America program are to evaluate each of three major methods of learning to read, according to its effectiveness with all children as well as with children having certain learning advantages or disabilities. Then the students are to formulate a plan for using two or more methods during their first year of teaching. This plan is to be judged plausible by a committee of three primary teachers, each of whom advocates or tends to emphasize a different method of teaching reading.

Evaluation

1. After developing criteria for appraising poetry—such as clarity of thought, meaningful imagery, and flow of ideas through appropriate use of rhyme, meter, and punctuation—seventh-grade students are to use these criteria in evaluating three poems selected by the teacher.

2. Following a course in reading improvement, high-school students are to indicate whether or not they have improved in (a) speed, (b) comprehension, (c) word-attack skills, (d) reading interests, (e) enjoyment of reading, and (f) facility in adjusting type of reading to the nature of the material and the purpose for reading it.

3. After establishing criteria for judging whether or not a given piece of literature is appropriate for and interesting to young children, adolescents, and adults, students in a twelfth-grade English class are to apply these criteria to the ten best-sellers of the year. The criteria, criteria-application procedures, and findings are to be reviewed by three English teachers and judged appropriate and satisfactory.

Creative Skills

In dealing with student reading behavior, teachers may be satisfied simply with literal comprehension of the material, or go a step further in expecting the student to learn to draw inferences from it. But beyond this, teachers can make a major contribution to the student's intellectual development by fostering creative responses to the ideas presented by the author. The reader brings himself to the printed page; he interprets what he reads on the basis of his own experience and himself infuses the words he sees with meaning. If students are to gain as much as possible from their reading, this process should be examined, and the nature of the reading encounter be altered or developed as necessary.

For these reasons, there should be some objectives in reading instruction that focus upon creative responses: the traits and skills of awareness; sensitivity to meaning, to possible inference, and to how the material relates to the many facets of one's life; adaptive flexibility; and expressional fluency. In fostering these traits and skills, teachers should consider the advisability of doing so in a multidimensional approach that involves interrelated experiences in listening, speaking, reading, and writing. Two behavioral objectives involving creative traits and skills are:

1. During or following the reading of a teacher-selected poem, pupils are to write down associations and special meanings that various portions of the poem have for them. This type of assignment is to be presented a number of times, until pupils see reading as a means for stimulating their own thoughts.
2. After reading descriptions of the same current event or historical event by five different writers, pupils are to identify at least three different means used to describe the event, such as a straight reporting of the facts; an interpretative review including a legalistic, political, sociological, or economic analysis of the event; or an innovative portrayal of the event.

Discussion Questions and Activities

Probably the best way of responding to most of the following questions and ideas is as a member of a small group. Hopefully, this group would be interested in exploring how children learn to read; new developments, thoughts, and understandings about teaching reading; sources of help in the teaching of reading; and ways of improving competencies in helping children learn to read and in improving their skill and enjoyment in reading. Discussions should lead to honest self-assessment and to development of personal plans for improving effectiveness in this essential area of the curriculum.

1. What is the major purpose of teaching children to read?

2. What do you consider the best method of teaching children to read?

3. What are the major strengths and weaknesses of the various methods?

4. What information on each child would be needed in order to be of the greatest help in teaching him to read? What are the best and most readily available sources for this information?

5. Discuss with four other teachers three techniques that seem to work best for you in teaching reading.

6. Review for a group of teachers one of the basic references in reading, one of the references for this unit, an article on reading prepared by a nationally-recognized authority in reading, or a research study.

7. What can teachers do to help children with special reading problems? Culturally disadvantaged children? Emotionally disturbed children? Neurologically handicapped children? Discuss these problems with a school psychologist.

8. What reading skills are needed especially in reading a poem? A biology textbook? An account of World War II? Is it possible to identify those reading skills that are emphasized most in each of the subject areas taught in high school and college?

9. In what ways should teachers help pupils to read in the different content fields in elementary and high school?

10. What might teachers do to provide a developmental and individualized reading program for children who are already reading by the time they enter kindergarten or first grade? What cautions should be observed?

11. Describe the hierarchy of reading development outlined in Ruth Strang's *Reading*.

12. Complete the following sentence: "Perceptual readiness for reading usually occurs . . ."

13. What is the relationship between intelligence and reading ability?

14. After reading Lawrence Carrillo's *Informal Reading-Readiness Experiences*, and sources on reading readiness, list five indications of reading readiness and three things teachers might do to foster each of these five items.

15. How can teachers improve their own reading? Develop with at least two other persons an individual plan for improving your own reading. How would you assess your current competencies and possibly discover certain areas that might be improved? What sort of regime or schedule would be reasonable for this type of self-assessment and improvement process? Describe the procedure you will use to determine whether or not your efforts at improvement have actually resulted in improvement.

16. In what ways is reading related to speaking? To listening? To writing?

Bibliography

Betts, Emmett Albert, ed. "Modern Approaches to Reading," *Education* 88 (April–May 1969): 291–330.

Bond, Guy L., and Tinker, Miles A. *Reading Difficulties: Their Diagnosis and Correction.* 2d ed. New York: Appleton-Century-Crofts, 1967.

Boning, Richard. "Locating the Answer" (1966); "Using the Context" (1962); "Following Directions" (1967); and "Getting the Facts" (1965). Rockville Centre, N.Y.: Barnell Loft.

Buktenica, Normal A. *Visual Learning.* San Rafael, Calif.: Dimensions Publishing, 1968.

Carrillo, Lawrence W. *Informal Reading-Readiness Experiences.* San Francisco: Chandler, 1964.

———. *Reading Institute Extension Services, K–6 and 7–12.* Chicago: Science Research Associates, 1969.

Chall, Jeanne. "Beginning Reading: Where Do We Go from Here?" *Today's Education* 2 (February 1969): 36–9.

———. *Learning to Read—The Great Debate.* New York: McGraw-Hill, 1967.

Clark County School District. *Reading and the Kindergarten Child.* Las Vegas: Clark County School District, 1968.

Cupertino Elementary School District. *Open-End Curriculum in 3R Subject,* rev. ed. Cupertino, Calif.: Cupertino Elementary School District, 1970.

De Boer, John J., and Dallman, Martha. *The Teaching of Reading.* New York: Holt, Rinehart & Winston, 1964.

Gray, William S. *On Their Own in Reading.* Chicago: Scott, Foresman, 1960.

Harris, Albert J. *How to Increase Reading Ability,* 5th ed. New York: David McKay Co., 1970.

Heilman, Arthur W. *Principles and Practices of Teaching Reading,* 2d ed. Columbus, Ohio: Charles E. Merrill, 1967.

Journal of Reading. Neward, Del.: International Reading Association. (All issues.)

Martin, Bill J. "Sounds of Language." Readers. New York: Holt, Rinehart & Winston, 1966.

Parker, Don H., and Scannell, Genevieve. *Reading Laboratory Series.* Chicago: Science Research Associates, 1969.

Reading for Understanding, rev. ed. Chicago: Science Research Associates, 1969.

Reading Research Quarterly. Newark, Del.: International Reading Association. (All issues.)

The Reading Teacher. Newark, Del.: International Reading Association. (All issues.)

Research for Better Schools, Inc. "Teaching in I.P.I. Mathematics" (A Program of Teacher Preparation) Vol. 1 of 6. Philadelphia: Research for Better Schools, 1969.

———. "Working Paper Number 30: Individually Prescribed Instruction." Philadelphia: Research for Better Schools, 1967.

Schubert, Delwyn G., and Torgerson, Theodore F. *Improving Reading Through Individualized Correction.* Dubuque, Iowa: William C. Brown, 1968.

Spache, George D. *Reading in the Elementary School.* Boston: Allyn & Bacon, 1964.

"Supplementary Teaching Plans." *SRA Basic Reading Series.* Chicago: Science Research Associates, 1968.

Stauffer, Russell G. *Directing Reading Maturity as a Cognitive Process.* New York: Harper & Row, 1969.

Strang, Ruth. *Diagnostic Teaching of Reading,* 2d ed. San Francisco: McGraw-Hill, 1969.

———. *Reading.* "Dimensions in Early Learning Series." San Rafael, Calif.: Dimensions Publishing, 1968.

Sullivan Associates. *Programed Reading.* Series I, II, III. St. Louis: McGraw-Hill, 1966.

Veatch, Jeannette. *Reading in the Elementary School.* New York: Ronald Press, 1966.

Woolman, Myron. *Reading in High Gear.* Chicago: Science Research Associates, 1965.

CHAPTER 8

ART AND MUSIC

8

Functions, Processes, and Skills of Art and Music

Art and Music in the Classroom

Academic Skills

Higher Cognitive Skills

Creative Skills

Craftsmanship Skills

Mankind creates art and music to express his life, his environment, and his dreams. From ancient to modern times, artists and musicians have helped to extend awareness and feeling, the fullness of living, and esthetic appreciation.

From the constant throb of the human heart
to the thunderous roar of a waterfall . . .
From jackhammer and pile driver biting and forcing
their way into concrete and soil
to the twittering sound of warblers
passing through on a spring migration . . .
From the menacing noise of war
to the purring of a kitten and the babbling
of a baby . . .
From the precise clicking and flashing
of a computer panel
to the lonely wail of a coyote . . .
the sounds and rhythms of life enmesh
and engulf us all in their web. And
in turnabout style, we reach out and
make these sounds a part of our being —
a part of our reality.

Through folksongs and symphonies and through billboards and masterpieces in oil, man records his reality and attempts to impose aspects of it upon another. Artistic experience may lead to an upswelling of ecstasy; it may trigger emotions of love and hate, tranquility and anxiety, sadness and joy. On the canvas or in the ballet, we see our real or intended selves. From the experience we may gravitate toward an ideal (beautiful or base) captured in artistic media and styles.

Around us today is constant evidence that man is manipulated by persons and organizations employing sounds and color, contrast and line, and artistic values and structures apparently scattered but deliberately situated throughout the dimensions of space and time.

Through a study of visual and auditory imagery we see more clearly man the manipulator and man the creator.

Art and music need not be merely the generalized background drapings and rhythms of our way of life. They may instead become highly significant, personal, and intimate aspects of our being, of what we represent,

and

of what we would become.

The choice is ours.

Functions, Processes, and Skills of Art and Music

If we would give meaning to sounds and objects, to words and mustic, and to paint or stone, we must know something about design, the nature of materials, tools, and instruments, and the technique of applying tools and instruments. This knowledge and understanding comes to teachers and pupils through experience; and one of the fundamental aspects of this experience is gaining some degree of craftsmanship, whether it be in paint, in wood or stone, or in words and tones.

The functions, processes, and skills of the fine arts include:

1. Cutting and shaping wood, stone, and synthetic material in order to portray an event or to express an idea
2. Arranging objects or representations of objects in two- or three-dimensional space—for example, drawing, painting, photographing, fabricating steel sculpture, mobiles and collages, interior decorating, architectural drawing, and city, community, and environmental planning
3. Composing and producing patterns of sound
4. Weaving together dance steps into esthetic patterns, and mixing these skillfully with sound and visual backdrops to produce a dance, a ballet, or an opera
5. Fashioning words into phrases, paragraphs, prose, and poetry
6. Creating plays and other dramatic presentations
7. Interweaving color, sound, pictures, words, dance, and music to create new multiple-impact forms of art

What Is Art?

Art is a means and media of representation, portrayal, or visual description. It is a process and product. It is made possible through functions, processes, and skills, and is made up of elements deployed by certain principles. Art includes all these things, plus the skills of analysis and appreciation, the products of the artist, the artist himself, art and music forms, and historical periods by which are classified artistic production.

In a discussion of art, music might well be considered concurrently with the other fine arts. But for the purposes of this chapter, the aural arts will be separated from the visual arts, although some art forms require a blending of both.

Appreciation requires depth of analysis, whether it be in recognizing a historical period or an artist's style, or in discerning the elements of a musician's composition. Analysis may lead to an understanding of how an artist or composer produces a work, fresh and vibrant, through the use of elements and principles, through attention to rhythm, harmony, and melody, and through his flooding or receding of hues and tones.

Art and Music in the Classroom

Why are art and music taught? Each person would answer this question a little differently. But perhaps it can be said at this point that art and music are taught:

1. To help a child become a better person
2. To provide a child with knowledge of the nature of art and music, techniques, artists and musicians, and historical periods
3. To develop a child's awareness and powers of discrimination, analysis, and evaluation
4. To help a child explore his feelings and to find himself
5. To prepare a child to choose from an array of promising, interesting, personally rewarding careers and avocations
6. To develop a child's commitment to the ideal of making the world a beautiful place in which to live, through having art and music in homes and communities
7. To help a child to create and to experience the joy of creating a thing of beauty

How Art and Music Are Taught

The manner in which art and music are taught is affected by the attitudes teachers have toward esthetic expression, toward children, and toward the curriculum. It is influenced by prescribed content and recommended procedures in learning sequences.

Some years ago, a little first-grade child brought home a ceramic object, handed it to his mother, and said, "Happy Mothers' Day. My teacher said you wouldn't like it." With greater sophistication than this teacher, we refrain from negative judgment that will dampen a child's enthusiasm and shut the door to his further creative efforts.

School settings are needed in which art and music abound —in pictures, sculpture, cultural artifacts, and all types of music. From initial exploratory experiences with certain media, artists, masterpieces, and pupil work, certain principles emerge. These in turn are used to guide further effort and development. Recognizing the personal meaning of art and creative production, the teacher refrains from asking a young child, "What's that?" Instead, he says, "Tell me about it." As skill and knowledge grow, so do the standards set for artistic production. Emphasis may be upon cultural enrichment, upon individual self-understanding, and, in some instances, upon rapid or flexible progression through content, skills, and experiences. In teaching art, discovery methods can be used that emphasize both convergent and divergent thought. The content of art instruction should be relevant to the learner—to his cultural background, his understanding, skill attainment, degree of craftsmanship, maturative needs, and phenomenological field.

Gauging Pupil Growth and Effectiveness

Probably the most effective instrument for judging artistic and musical performance is the skilled teacher, who is himself accomplished in some area of artistic expression. However, facts, concepts, and generalizations can be effectively assessed by teacher-made and publisher-produced tests.

Certain artistic aptitude and ability tests, and certain creativity tests may be appropriately used to gain some indication of likely success in painting or in playing a musical instrument; in judging the esthetic qualities of a particular sound or visual composition; or in developing such traits of creativity as originality, flexibility, and fluency. Because many of these measures are still at a preliminary or field-testing stage of development, evaluation should not be restricted to the use of these instruments.

Review

The need for behavioral or performance objectives is obvious, as is the fact that we must be precise in stating goals and in determining how to judge whether they have been reached. This is as true in art and music as it is in science and mathematics. We should know what a child is expected to gain from school-sponsored experiences and how he might be expected to change or improve his attitudes, interests, knowledge, and skills.

Before studying behavioral objectives in art and music, these questions should be considered:

1. What is art?
2. Of what value are art and music to children and adults?
3. List and describe basic elements and principles of music and the visual arts.
4. Compare the elements and principles of painting with those of composing a piece of music.
5. In your judgment, what are the most defensible ways to teach art and music at each level of the elementary school, junior high school, and high school?
6. Develop a checklist of behaviors which you think children should be able to accomplish at one or more of the above-mentioned grade levels. Compare this list with one developed by a fellow teacher. Do you differ basically as to when you would teach or the sequencing of teaching concepts or certain skills?
7. List four distinguishing characteristics of behavioral objectives.

Academic Skills

In framing academic skill objectives, this section is concerned with art elements, principles, tools, and materials; artists; art history; and great works of art. Attention will also be given to musical elements, forms, and instruments; musicians; history of music; and great musical compositions.

Art

Academic behavioral skill objectives in art emphasize concepts and understandings that are a part of one's cultural heritage. As such, they merit the attention both of persons wanting a general understanding of art and of students contemplating careers in one of a number of artistic or art-related fields. Examples of academic behavioral objectives are:

1. Following a study of the elements and principles of art, sixth-grade students are to identify to the satisfaction of

their teacher the art elements and principles employed in
one or more paintings by Vincent van Gogh, Leonardo da
Vinci, Piet Mondrian, and John Singer Sargent.

2. Ninty-five percent of the pupils in a fifth-grade class are to
   view colored slides of twenty famous paintings and indicate without error which paintings are impressionistic,
   realistic, or abstract.
3. To demonstrate their ability to recognize the Greek,
   Corinthian, Doric, and Ionic orders of architecture, students are to identify correctly the order illustrated by five
   Greek buildings or ruins and five American buildings. This
   objective is to be pursued following an assignment in
   which children make clay models of each type of column.
4. In a test given after a unit on famous art and artists, children in a seventh-grade class are to match, with no more
   than three errors, a list of fifteen artists with a list of their
   paintings.
5. Within a forty-five minute period, students in eleventh-
   grade art are to write papers on "American Architecture
   since 1870." The papers are to contain information on
   changes in style, principles of construction, and materials
   used. Eighty-five percent of the students should successfully complete this assignment.
6. Following a visit to an art museum, or after seeing a film
   or slides on art through the ages, each fourth-grade pupil
   is to identify three paintings he likes and three he does not
   like and give reasons for his choices. Reasons given are to
   reflect the individual's own values or a set of external
   standards used by teachers in selecting art prints for display in elementary-school classrooms.

Music

Following are examples of academic skill behavioral objectives in music:

1. After reading appropriate reference books, students are to
   write correct definitions for four basic elements of music—
   harmony, melody, rhythm, and tone color—and then to
   illustrate these elements by singing or playing portions of
   recordings. Eighty percent of the students are to provide
   illustrations that a trained music teacher verifies are
   accurate and clear examples.
2. To demonstrate that they know the major instruments of
   the orchestra, fourth-grade pupils are to view a display of
   musical instruments and correctly identify on a checklist
   seven out of nine instruments.

3. Following a study of the composition of an orchestra, students complete a ten-minute quiz in which they correctly identify the four choirs of the orchestra (woodwind, string, brass, and percussion), and, with no more than two errors, list the names of two woodwind instruments, three brass instruments, two percussion instruments, and three string instruments.

4. Students match with no more than three errors a list of fifteen composers and a list of twenty-five musical compositions. Sixth-grade students are to complete this assignment within a ten-minute period. This assignment is to be made upon concluding a three-week study of musicians and musical compositions.

5. To develop and demonstrate analytical ability, fifth-grade pupils are to listen to two symphonies and then are to write 200- to 400-word critiques in which they indicate (a) prominent instruments; (b) variations in speed and volume; and (c) effects created by instrumentation, tempo, and dynamics.

6. In a dramatic play concerning life on the American frontier in 1850, fifth-grade students are to sing from memory three pioneer songs. After five practice sessions, seventy-five percent of the students in the class are to make no more than three errors in words of the songs.

7. Advanced eleventh-grade music students are to define twelve of the following terms correctly:

plain chant	overture
a capella	adagio
meistersingers	allegro
harpsichord	symphony
polyphonic	virtuoso
baroque music	leitmotif
fugue	blues
homophonic	fortissimo
oratorio	diatonic
recitative	glockenspiel

Definitions are to be compared with those in a dictionary of musical terms. This is to be done to the satisfaction of the teacher.

8. Students compare the works of Dvorak, Grieg, and Sibelius and indicate at least one way in which Dvorak differed from the other two composers in the choice of subject for his music. This objective is to be carried out after a one-week period in which students listen to and take notes on the music and lives of these three composers.

Higher Cognitive Skills

Intellectual or cognitive aspects of art and music can be emphasized in historical studies, appreciation courses, and advanced programs that help the skilled performer or student analyze sound and visual composition. This analysis may serve as a basis for creations of original works. The application of principles to new situations and new encounters with sound, line, and color also is a higher cognitive skill. Finally, the establishment of a rational basis for evaluating masterpieces of previous eras, contemporary works, and one's own work represent these upper-level skills.

Cognitive skills are sharpened in some schools where even fourth- and fifth-grade pupils discuss intelligently the elements and principles of art used by artists in the production of masterpieces, and when pupils use established standards and their own predilections and values to evaluate these same paintings. Productive divergent thinking skills are enhanced when students are encouraged to propose an array of possible solutions to a problem of artistic design. Likewise, in the choice of music to create a certain mood or effect, students might listen to and then select from a number of pieces those that most fittingly would be part of a concert or a preholiday program of music and drama.

Art

Some behavioral objectives that highlight and enhance higher cognitive skills are:

1. Given access to books and displays on design, fabric texture, color, and room arrangement, each seventh-grade homemaking student is to prepare a plan for making one room of his home more attractive. Plans are to be judged on the basis of established principles of interior decoration agreed upon in advance by students and their teacher. Judges are to include a professional interior decorator and two parents, or the school principal and two parents. *(Interpretation)*

2. To read, discover, and outline reasons for the gain or loss in popularity of certain paintings, the student is to read teacher-recommended selections from three references in art history and art appreciation. Reasons given are to include those advanced by authorities in art and those formulated by the student. The latter must be considered plausible by the teacher or by a panel of three art students. *(Analysis and interpretation)*

3. Pupils are to consider for five minutes the questions: "What is good art?" and "What is bad art?" They are then to form five-person discussion groups. During a twenty-minute period, each pupil is to present one criterion of good art; the criterion is to be accepted in its original or in a modified form, and incorporated into a list of criteria of good art developed by the group. *(Synthesis and interpretation)*

4. Presented with reproductions of fifteen famous paintings, the pupil is to identify correctly twelve of these paintings for the following styles: baroque, romanticism, realism, impressionism, cubism, surrealism, and abstract-impressionism. *(Analysis)*

5. Having developed criteria for judging art, students are to apply their criteria to paintings on display in a local art gallery, to paintings done by members of the class, and to portfolios of art reproductions. Each student is to judge ten paintings and to indicate which painting he likes best and which least. *(Evaluation)*

6. Pupils select and mount five pictures illustrating how they felt while reading a certain book, while alone in a house or outside on a windy day, when frightened by a storm, or when happily surprised. This is to be done during an art period or as homework over a two-day period. *(Interpretation)*

7. Following a period of listening to any classical or modern musical composition, pupils paint or draw pictures with color, form, line, and arrangement of symbols or objects to reflect the mood induced by the music. *(Interpretation)*

8. Using any art tools and media, each student creates a painting, woodcarving, or other object that seventy-five percent of the students in the class can identify as religious or secular, tranquil or disturbing, realistic or abstract. *(Interpretation)*

9. After learning the principles and techniques of crayon batik or tempera design, students create wall-hangings or pictures or designs to decorate the school room or rooms in their homes. Ninety percent of the participating pupils should merit the grade of C (average), or B (good), or A (outstanding) for the application of principles or for their technique in creating a wall-hanging, design, or picture. *(Application)*

Music

Higher cognitive skill objectives in music might be formulated from such ingredients as historical periods, forms, principles, elements, composers, performers, and compositions. The intellectual aspects of music and art can lead students to greater understanding and challenge, but they can also produce a deadening effect upon interest, enthusiasm, and creativity. Because of this, a student should not only be exposed to intellectual encounters, but he should also be immersed in congruent fields of sound that will educate the attending, responding, and valuing aspects of his being. Part of the total experience may involve another dimension, that of actual performance. In this way, both the interpretation and production of music become part of a pupil's kinesthetic memory and his reservoir of response patterns. Examples of higher cognitive skill objectives follow:

1. After listening to or singing three songs, pupils in a third-grade class are to tell the teacher what they like or do not like about the songs. Each pupil is to make at least one response that the teacher can use in helping the class develop a set of criteria for evaluating music. *(Evaluation)*

2. With the aid of an oscilloscope and an eight-millimeter camera, or with an oscillograph, students in a twelfth-grade physics class are to identify and record the visible waves produced by portions of five musical compositions. After studying the wave variations (the fingerprints of sound), students in the class are to identify the musical compositions solely by their wave variations. *(Analysis)*

3. In describing an unfamiliar musical composition, students in a ninth-grade music class are to use correctly, according to an authoritative reference book, the terms *rhythm, melody, harmony,* and *tone color and form. (Application)*

4. With the help of the orchestra or band teacher, an advanced music student is to play the same piece of music *andante, allegretto, allegro,* and *adagio;* and *pianissimo* and *forte.* He is then to take a survey of the emotional impact of the different variations. This is to be done by playing a tape recording to three classes of fifth-grade students and having them record on a questionnaire how the variations affected them. A report on results of the survey is to be made. All portions of the assignment are to be judged satisfactory by members of the high school music department. *(Analysis and synthesis)*

5. Using all available library references and consulting two or more adults, the student is to list ten criteria for judging the worth of a given musical composition. These criteria are to be easily understood by at least seventy percent of the students in a seventh-grade English or social studies class. This determination is to be made with the help of a teacher. *(Synthesis)*

6. Those students who have studied German for two years in high school are to translate the words of a common German song. This is to be done to the satisfaction of the German teacher. *(Translation)*
7. Students working on a special project in music appreciation are to translate correctly sixty percent of the notations on an orchestral score. *(Translation)*
8. After listening to three musical selections, fourth-grade pupils indicate whether or not the composers were creating sad, happy, pastoral, or exciting moods. These determinations are to be judged plausible by a panel of three students. *(Interpretation)*
9. To determine the musical instrument or form of musical expression associated with particular composers, students are to consult two or more references on music history, biographies, and encyclopedias. *(Analysis)*

Creative Skills

Children and adults alike may be so in awe of the great masterpieces of art and music that they feel creativity to be the sold province of the Michelangelos, the da Vincis, and the Beethovens. If this were true, we might indeed ask, "Why should we consider creative skill objectives as guides in the education of all children?" The answer to this question can be found in the way we define creativity, in our expectancies of children, and in how children respond to and benefit from creative experiences in art and music.

Creativity may be thought of as an attitude or a process for extending awareness, for overcoming obstacles to thinking and doing, and for producing original and worthwhile products. Through art the teacher helps a child to see the world and himself in clearer perspective. With newly acquired skills of visual discrimination and of representation, the child becomes able to record, portray, and synthesize impressions in new and meaningful ways.

Art and music may help a child to become more sensitive and aware. They may also provide affective emotional experiences and esthetic experiences that motivate the child toward achievement, toward maturity, toward seeing beauty, and toward joyful living. Art and music may be the means of helping a person to escape from the world for a time and to involve himself solely in viewing, listening, playing, or creating; to gain a new perspective of roles, problems, and work; to manipulate concepts; and, possibly, to acquire renown for contributing to the world a thing of beauty or an artistic creation with a message for one's day or for all mankind.

Art

Behavioral objectives in art, such as those following, might help the child to become more aware of his world or to create objects of art:

1. After using a woodcarving tool to make figures or bowls with five different types of wood, ninth-grade students are to list the properties of each type of wood that make it desirable or undesirable for carving. Each student should list at least one property for each type of wood that he used. *(Awareness)*

2. Through experiences in mixing and using watercolors, primary children are to learn to distinguish between primary and secondary colors and three different hues of each primary color. *(Awareness)*

3. To describe ways in which color is used by artists, advertisers, and interior decorators to create effects, students are to read parts of a book about the psychology of color, parts of two books on preparing advertisements, and parts of two books on interior decorating. The students' descriptions are to be in the form of a theme or an illustrated notebook. *(Awareness)*

4. Each pupil in a second-grade class is to bring a flower to school or to select one from a bouquet brought by the teacher. Following a period of discussion about the color, texture, and shape of the various parts of the flower, each child should indicate to the teacher at least three things that he learned about his flower. *(Awareness)*

5. Using dried corn, peas, and beans, second-grade pupils are to make a mosaic with white glue and cardboard. Seventy-five percent of the pupils are to create mosaics that they elect to wrap and present to their parents as gifts. *(Originality)*

6. Within a forty-five minute art period, eighty-five percent of the pupils in a fourth grade are to create a yarn collage, paper mosaic, sumi brush painting, soap carving, paper sculpture, sponge painting, paper mobile, waxed paper and tissue lamination, or cotton painting. *(Originality)*

Music

Music as well as art is a medium through which a child may express himself and grow to become more sensitive, flexible, fluent, and original in his expression. Behavioral objectives in music might be formulated to foster the following traits of creativity: sensitivity, awareness, flexibility, fluency, and originality.

Craftsmanship Skills

Distinguishing characteristics of a skilled craftsman are (1) careful attention to and appropriateness of design, (2) knowledge of the unique properties of materials, (3) selection and proper care of tools, and (4) skillful use of tools and materials in creating a beautiful, useful, accurate, or worthwhile product. Also important is the ability to assess an object of art.

Art

Examples of craftsmanship behavioral objectives in art are:

1. Using shopping bags, tempera paints, crayon, glue, cardboard, and yarn, pupils are to plan and fashion Halloween or Mayan masks which they wear comfortably at a class party or in a skit or play.
2. Following a study of the properties of wood and functions of different carving tools, ninth-grade students are to select appropriate types of wood and proper tools for carving a bowl, a design on a wood panel, or a figure of a mountain climber or ballet dancer.
3. During a clean-up period, students are to demonstrate efficient and appropriate techniques for removing all evidence of latex and oil paint from nylon and natural bristle brushes. An inspection of the brushes by the teacher should reveal no evidence of paint.
4. Before beginning an individual art project, students are to take an art test in which they identify three or more favorable properties and three or more limitations of clay, plasticene, plaster of paris, and cement as media.
5. To demonstrate the skills of drawing to scale, lettering, using certain architectural symbols, reading a simple floor plan, and arranging furniture, eleventh-grade art and home-economics students are to prepare a scale drawing of a living room, bedroom, or kitchen; establish their own arrangement of furniture; indicate doors, windows, and fireplaces; and with legible and neat lettering label each room. A panel of students and the teacher are to judge each of the drawings. Students who have averaged an "A" during five months of work in art and home economics should have their drawings chosen for display.

6. Without any assistance from the teacher, fourth-grade pupils are to select an appropriate glaze to give a certain effect to a three-dimensional ceramic product that is both decorative and functional. After firing, nine out of ten products should create the desired effect.

7. In making costume jewelry, ninety percent of the pupils are to receive a satisfactory rating for design, selection of materials, and safe and skillful use of three or more tools.

8. To show knowledge of the unique properties of watercolor, oils, and acrylic paints, students are to define their characteristics in a discussion with the teacher or in three written paragraphs, and to paint three pictures, each one highlighting the properties of a particular medium.

9. Upon demonstrating his skill in coil construction and slab building, every fifth-grade pupil is to be judged an apprentice or craftsman on the basis of criteria developed and established by both the teacher and pupils. One of these criteria might be the degree of self-direction shown by that pupil. Pupils judged to be at or above the eightieth percentile in manual dexterity and practical problem-solving should receive the craftsman rating. To achieve this rating, they would have to be judged above average on seven or more behaviors encompassing the areas of design, use of materials, selection and care of tools, and skillful use of tools and materials.

Discussion Questions and Activities

1. What is art? Why has it always been a part of man's life?

2. Is art a method for documenting reality? A means of recording events, places, and things? A way of sharing feelings of emotion and joy in appreciating or producing a thing of beauty?

3. How might teachers best approach the study of art? Should our concern be mainly with developing budding artists and advancing career goals in art, or with developing art appreciation and cultural enrichment? Should our approach be historical, analytical, technical, expressional, or existential? Should we look at art from the vantage points and with the tools of psychology, sociology, or anthropology?

4. Discuss the following: Realizing that there may be merit to all of the above-mentioned approaches, we might propose to deal with art in some established sequence based upon maturity factors and skill-development, or we might propose a multidimensional or comprehensive study of art in which the approaches or perspectives might be woven together in a mutually supporting manner. What should be the organizational pattern of art instruction or of the art curriculum?

5. Certainly important are the highly personal experiences in artistic expression. To achieve these experiences, a degree of privacy in work must be assured. Important, too, are experiences which help students to see the relationship of art and music, the value of art to the individual, and the relationships of art to other portions of the curriculum, such as mathematics, science, history, and literature. What has your school or school system done or what might it do to foster ideas such as these?

6. Of what value is the study of music? What are some specific benefits accruing from a study of music? How might music become the basis for enrichment activities in science and mathematics? What specific steps might your school or school district take to give students appropriate experiences in music?

Bibliography

Art Education. Washington: National Art Education Association. (All issues.)

Brown, Robert B., and Troth, Eugene W. Music 100: An Introduction to Music History. New York: American Book, 1967.

Canaday, John. Metropolitan Seminars in Art. New York: Metropolitan Museum of Art, 1958.

Chase, Alice Elizabeth. Famous Paintings: An Introduction to Art for Young Readers. New York: Platt & Munk, 1962.

Christensen, Fred. Recipes for Creative Art. Monterey Park, Calif.: Creative Teaching Press, 1967.

Copland, Aaron. What to Listen For in Music. New York: McGraw-Hill, 1957.

Glendale Unified School District. Art Guide. Glendale, Calif.: Glendale Unified School District, 1966.

Grosser, Maurice. The Painter's Eye. New York: Mentor Books, 1955.

Linderman, Earl W., and Herberholz, Donald W. Developing Artistic and Perceptual Awareness. Dubuque, Iowa: Brown, 1964.

Linscott, Robert N., ed. The Notebooks of Leonardo da Vinci. Abridged. Translated by Edward MacCurdy. New York: The Modern Library, 1957.

Marksberry, Mary Lee. Foundations of Creativity. New York: Harper & Row, 1963.

New York State Department of Education. The Humanities: A Planning Guide for Teachers. Edited by William R. Clauss. Albany, N.Y.:

Bureau of Secondary Curriculum Development, The University of the State of New York.

Obler, Paul C. Mirrors of Man: A Reader for Composition and Humanities. New York: American Book, 1962.

Randolph, David. This Is Music: A Guide to the Pleasures of Listening. New York: Mentor Books, 1965.

Wechsberg, Joseph. The Pantheon Story of Music for Young People. New York: Random House, 1968.

CHAPTER 9

HEALTH

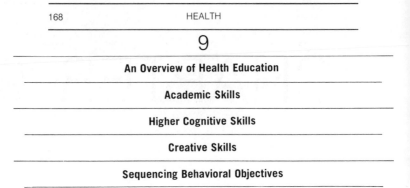

9

An Overview of Health Education

Academic Skills

Higher Cognitive Skills

Creative Skills

Sequencing Behavioral Objectives

Schools help students improve the quality of their lives through teaching them how to improve and maintain their physical and emotional health. Perhaps in no other area of the curriculum is learning so directly applicable to the everyday life of the individual. The purposes of health education are of vital importance not only to the individual but also to the society of which he is a part.

An Overview of Health Education

The purpose of health instruction is to provide the individual with positive health attitudes and practices and a range of skills that can help him solve individual and community health problems. The health of the child is requisite to his success in school and, perhaps more importantly, to his success as a functional and productive member of society. The magnitude of existing health problems and the ever-increasing body of scientific and medical knowledge to be interpreted make health instruction a necessity.

The Content of Health Instruction

Health instruction is more than the study of hygiene, growth, and posture. It is concerned with much more than the dissemination of knowledge about human physiology and anatomical structures. Because the goals of health instruction include the solving of individual and community health problems, the substantive matter of the health curriculum must be based upon the health needs of children and youth and of society.

Health instruction is an applied science in which information from the behavioral and biological sciences is used to the extent that it will help the learner to understand and solve pertinent health problems. In health instruction, the facts and principles relative to anatomy, physiology, biology, and the behavioral sciences are means to an end, rather than ends in themselves. The essential element of health instruction consists of the facts and principles pertaining to healthful living. These facts and principles can be organized into the following health content areas: [1]

Consumer Health: Concerns selection and utilization of health services, information, and products; health fads and fallacies; and quackery.

Mental-Emotional Health: Includes promotion and maintenance of good mental health, factors influencing mental health, and prevention and treatment of mental illness.

Drug Use and Abuse: Emphasizes values of positive use of drugs and dangers of misuse, factors that influence drug abuse, and means of prevention and control of drug abuse.

Family Health: Encompasses factors that contribute to successful family living, roles of family members, reproduction and the reproductive system, and growth and development characteristics of children and adolescents.

Oral Health: Relates effects of oral neglect and the prevention and treatment of oral disorders.

Vision and Hearing: Stresses protection and maintenance of good vision and hearing and the prevention and treatment of common disorders.

Nutrition: Concerns importance of good nutrition; effects of poor nutrition; nutritional needs of children, adolescents, and adults; and food fads and fallacies.

Exercise, Rest, and Posture: Emphasizes benefits of a balanced program of exercise and rest; fitness needs of children, youth, and adults; and the importance of good posture.

Diseases and Disorders: Includes factors that contribute to diseases and disorders, effects of diseases and disorders, and prevention and control of chronic and communicable diseases.

Environmental Health Hazards: Stresses problems in man's environment that pose a threat to his health, such as air and water pollution, noise, pesticides, radiation, food additives, and ways of solving such problems.

---

1. For a more detailed analysis of these areas, see *Framework for Health Instruction in California Public Schools,* compiled by John T. Fodor, Ben C. Gmur, and Wilfred C. Sutton (Sacramento: California State Department of Education, 1970).

Safety and Accident Prevention: Includes factors contributing to accidents, the prevention and control of accidents, and emergency procedures in case of accidents.

Community Health Resources: Concerns health resources available in our society and the benefits of such resources to the individual and to society. In each of the content areas just described, the learner is expected to acquire basic concepts or principles appropriate to his grade level and particular learning needs.

How Health Is Taught

The effective teaching of health requires an active involvement in creating, shaping, and adjusting learning opportunities to meet the specific needs of students. Specified behavioral objectives are essential to the fulfillment of health goals, and the learning opportunities involved might include the use of educational media such as books, pamphlets, periodicals, bulletin boards, chalkboards, flannel boards, films, filmstrips, pictures, recordings, and slides. To help students solve individual and community health problems, the health teacher should also provide learning situations that include group and individual activities, such as brainstorming sessions, small and large group discussion, field trips, lectures, panel discussions, problem-solving or question-and-answer periods, self-appraisals, role-playing, and symposia or reports.

The teaching of health should not be a one-way process, whereby the teacher disseminates knowledge and the student passively absorbs it. Rather, health instruction should be considered a dynamic process involving the interaction of student and teacher.

Gauging Pupil Growth and Effectiveness

In health instruction, the process of evaluation is a continuous one. It begins before the instruction period, when the needs of students must be identified as a basis for the content to be taught. As the instruction continues evaluation is necessary to gauge progress made toward the instructional objectives, and is then needed to determine, at the close of the instruction, how well the objectives have been attained.

In evaluating student progress, two techniques are used: (1) *clinical or subjective evaluation,* and (2) *statistical or objective evaluation.* Clinical or subjective evaluation is used primarily as a means for assessing the attainment of health attitudes and practices. Techniques that may be employed include observations, checklists, anecdotal records, questionnaires, interviews, self-appraisals, sociodramas, and small group discussions. Observation is the primary technique used in this type of evaluation. The additional techniques noted are useful for increasing the reliability of observations.

Statistical or objective evaluation is accomplished by paper-and-pencil tests, and is used primarily to assess the attainment of cognitive skills. Tests may utilize objective items, such as true-false, multiple-choice, matching, or fill-in questions. Other tests may be composed of essay-type questions, which are used primarily to assess the attainment of higher-level cognitive skills.

For the greatest effectiveness, a combination of evaluative techniques should be employed; it is the teacher's responsibility to determine which techniques are most appropriate for each objective.

Academic Skills

If the goals of health instruction are to be met, students must be provided with opportunities to think clearly about ways to solve individual and community health problems. A range of academic skills must be identified including (1) acquisition of knowledge, (2) development of positive health attitudes, and (3) application of knowledge and attitudes in practices intended to prevent or solve individual and community health problems.

Knowledge Skills

Examples of behavioral objectives stressing knowledge skills are given for each of the health content areas:

Consumer Health

1. Eighth-grade students are to study a magazine advertisement about a health product and identify three appeals used in the advertisement to persuade the consumer to purchase that product.
2. Each student is to write a list of at least four criteria for selecting and using health products, following reading and discussion on this subject.
3. Given an example of a community health problem and a list containing job descriptions of health advisors, and using criteria established in class discussions, students in a tenth-grade health class are to select the health advisor most qualified to help correct that particular health problem.

4. After a period of observing health-product commercials on TV, each tenth-grade student writes a commercial illustrating three techniques used to motivate the consumer to buy a product. These techniques are those previously identified and discussed by the teacher.

5. Within a five-minute period, all students in a tenth-grade health class distinguish on a list of ten statements about health products those that are facts from those that are fallacies. Responses should be in accordance with information in an authoritative text on health.

Mental-Emotional Health

1. After hearing a talk by a school psychologist, ninth-grade students are to select from a list of ten terms six that are proposed by one or more authorities in mental health as characteristics of good mental health in adolescents.

2. After viewing a film showing a stressful situation, the student chooses from a list of eight responses prepared by the teacher three that would reduce stress in that situation.

3. Students are to describe orally or in writing three ways in which environmental factors influence mental health and three ways in which biological factors influence mental health. Descriptions should be in accordance with those found in an authoritative text.

4. Each student in a tenth-grade health class is to write an example showing how each of four given environmental factors can positively or negatively influence a person's behavior. Examples given must be substantiated by at least one authoritative reference.

5. Within a five-minute period tenth-grade students correctly define orally or in writing each of the following terms: *fantasy, rationalization, projection,* and *regression.* Within an additional fifteen-minute period students describe situations in which each mental mechanism is used. This is to be accomplished after they have studied and discussed mental adjustment mechanisms.

Drug Use and Abuse

1. The student is to identify on a list of medicines compiled by the teacher those that require a prescription from a physician. Responses are to be verified by a school nurse.

2. After instruction on the effects of drugs, the student states three reasons, established by one or more medical authorities, why individuals can react differently to the same drug.

3. Each student in a tenth-grade health class states two immediate and two long-range effects of at least three drugs

on a list of five drugs. His statements must be substantiated with at least one authoritative reference.

4. Within a fifteen-minute period, each student in an eighth-grade health class explains one beneficial use of five out of ten medicines on a teacher-prepared list. Explanations should be in accordance with an authoritative text.

5. Without the aid of references, and following class discussion, tenth-grade students state orally or in writing examples of emotional factors that might lead to drug abuse.

Family Health

1. Students are to describe five areas of adjustment that may be considered necessary for a successful marriage. This is to be accomplished after the students read appropriate reference materials.

2. When provided with a list of growth and development characteristics, the student prepares a written report comparing changes that occur in boys and in girls during adolescence.

3. After study of reproductive systems, students correctly identify structures on a chart illustrating female and male reproductive systems.

4. After an introductory lesson on the sex drive, the student can state orally two reasons, documented by one or more authorities in the field, why the sex drive is important.

5. Given the names of four hormones involved in the menstrual cycle, the student correctly identifies the function of each hormone.

Oral Health

1. Using a list of dental and para-dental personnel, the student correctly classifies each by his specific role.

2. Each student in an eighth-grade health class correctly states an efficient and economical means of providing fluoride. Students are to give valid reasons for their choices and support their reasons by referring to one or more authoritative references.

3. Students in a tenth-grade health class, after reading pertinent information, describe orally or in writing three possible systemic effects of oral neglect.

4. The student is to identify from a list of health practices four practices helpful in preventing tooth decay that are suggested by the American Medical Association.

5. Students are to list two factors that one or more authorities say may contribute to hearing defects. This is to be done following the completion of a unit on hearing.

6. Upon being provided with a hypothetical situation in which the circumstances leading to a hearing problem are described, the student chooses from a teacher-prepared list three specific practices that might have prevented the problem.

Nutrition

1. Students correctly name the vitamins or minerals that a medical doctor would use to correct four diseases on a list of five provided by the teacher. Responses are judged correct if they are in accordance with recommendations of the American Medical Association.
2. Each student in a tenth-grade health class correctly differentiates facts from fallacies on a list of statements about food.
3. Given a breakfast menu that is deficient in foods from one of the four basic food groups, students correctly identify which food group is not represented.
4. Each student in a seventh-grade health class is to write a two-page paper concerning reasons vitamin supplements should not be taken indiscriminately. Three reasons given by the American Medical Association should be included in each paper.

Exercise, Rest, and Posture

1. Students are to arrange, in descending order of importance, a list of physical activities according to the caloric demand of each activity. This is to be done following a lesson about the caloric demands of various physical activities.
2. The student is to correctly identify from a series of pictures of various postural defects those that depict kyphosis, lordosis, and scoliosis.
3. Eighth-grade students are to classify as isometric or isotonic a list of exercises provided by the teacher.
4. Without the aid of references, the student gives one example of an isometric exercise and one example of an isotonic exercise, following instruction on various kinds of physical exercise. Each student also gives two values and two limitations of each exercise, in accordance with views held by one or more medical authorities.

Diseases and Disorders

1. Seventh-grade students are able to list each step on the infectious disease cycle. They do this following a period of instruction on communicable diseases.

2. With the aid of one or more references, the student is to list at least one symptom for each of five diseases listed on the chalkboard by the teacher.
3. After hearing a presentation of those factors considered by the Public Health Department to contribute to communicable disease, the student is able to list three of them.
4. Utilizing a Public Health Department list of steps necessary to prevent and control diseases and disorders, the student explains the purposes of each step.
5. All students in a seventh-grade health class are to identify on a list of diseases those for which a vaccine has been developed. This is to be accomplished following two days of instruction on immunization.
6. As the result of instruction on immunization, students write one-page papers describing the differences between active and passive immunity. At least three distinct features of each kind of immunity are to be cited in each paper.

Environmental Health Hazards

1. The student describes at least one environmental hazard created by each industrial process and scientific discovery or invention on a list distributed by the teacher.
2. Following a study of the effects of air pollution on health, each student prepares a five-paragraph paper in which he describes four health hazards caused by smog.
3. After a study of pollution of the environment, fifth-grade pupils are to list two ways of reducing water pollution, two ways of reducing air pollution, and three values of a clean environment.
4. Given a description of environmental conditions in a community, the student explains how two of the conditions can influence the emotional well-being of persons in that community.

Safety and Accident Prevention

1. Students identify on a list provided by the teacher health practices that reduce the risk of accidents. Choices should be in accordance with recommendations of the National Safety Council.
2. Twelfth-grade students are to write a two-page paper analyzing any one of four hypothetical accident situations posed by the teacher. The analysis is to include one emotional factor, one environmental factor, and one biological factor that contributed to the accident and what steps could have been taken to prevent the accident.

3. Given the description of an injury resulting from a hypothetical accident, the student can describe and demonstrate appropriate emergency procedures in accordance with those suggested by the American Red Cross.
4. Using a list of occupations provided by the teacher, students describe two types of accidents frequently associated with each occupation.

Community Health Resources

1. After receiving instruction on the services provided by the public health department, the student states orally four functions of this agency. Responses should be confirmed by a public health worker or school nurse.
2. Sixth-grade students are to list three community agencies and three international agencies that provide health services. This is to be accomplished following two days of instruction concerning health resources.
3. Students are to write four-paragraph papers explaining four ways in which they can help support community health services.
4. Tenth-grade students are to write five-page papers describing two health problems currently prevalent in society and the services necessary to help reduce these problems. The health problems identified must be substantiated by one or more authoritative references. Services to be provided must meet criteria established by the class.

Health Attitudes

Health attitudes reflect the values a student places on health, the degree to which he desires to carry out health practices or solve health problems, and his willingness to learn about such practices. It is difficult to measure the degree of attainment of objectives in this area. The stated criteria for the successful attainment of attitudinal behavioral objectives might even be limiting, because the student could demonstrate an attitude in ways other than those specified. In spite of these limitations, the inclusion of attitudinal objectives can add an important dimension to the health program.

Examples of behavioral objectives in the academic skill area of health attitudes follow:

Community Health Resources

1. After having one week of instruction on the services of official and voluntary health agencies, eighth-grade students, when given the opportunity, offer their services as student volunteers.

2. Students visit on their own a public health department and talk with a staff member about services provided. This interest is to be an outgrowth of receiving instruction on communicable-disease control.
3. Given a list of suggested reading topics, the student expresses his interest in health by selecting those topics relating to individual or community health.
4. The student expresses a desire to work in health-oriented occupations.

Drug Use and Abuse

1. The student indicates his desire to learn more about controlling drug abuse by voluntarily reading at least one supplemental article and one book on the subject.

Diseases and Disorders

1. Fifty percent of the students who have received one week of instruction on the control of chronic diseases indicate by supportive comments that they value the work of volunteer agencies that are attempting to eradicate diseases.

Environmental Health Hazards

1. Tenth-grade students display an interest in the problem of air pollution by bringing to class at least three magazine or newspaper articles on the subject.

Safety and Accident Prevention

1. One-third of the students in the tenth grade, who have received instruction in the area of automobile safety, express their interest in improving safety equipment in autos by voluntarily writing to a major auto company to inquire about steps the company is taking to improve the safety of its products.
2. In play situations on the school grounds, the student demonstrates his appreciation for the rights of others by practicing fair play and by showing that he is mindful of the health and safety of other students.

Health-Practice Objectives

Health-practice skills are the applicable principles of health knowledge. Although many of these involve higher cognitive skills, they are primarily concerned with information about health, and its application. Some health practices may be observed immediately in the school setting, even though many can be demonstrated only at home or in the community, or at some future date. Examples of health practice objectives that can be observed within the school setting follow:

Nutrition

1. When eating in the cafeteria, the student consistently chooses a balanced meal that contains foods from each of the four basic food groups.
2. Students choose fruit or fruit juices instead of candy when given an opportunity to buy snacks.

Communicable Diseases

1. Following instruction on the control of communicable diseases, third-grade students place hankerchiefs or tissues over their mouths every time they sneeze or cough.
2. Students in the second grade wash their hands after using the lavatory and before having meals. This should occur consistently after the students have had one week of instruction on controlling communicable diseases.
3. On rainy or cold days, each student wears appropriate protective clothing.

Mental-Emotional Health

1. Students indicate good human relations practices by introducing themselves and others to a new student, and by eating lunch with him.
2. In the fourth-grade classroom, the student consistently demonstrates practices conducive to making friends by being friendly, fair, and respectful of the rights of others.

Exercise, Rest, and Posture

1. Seventh-grade students participate in recreational or athletic activities after school at least three times a week.
2. After watching demonstrations of correct posture by the teacher, the student consistently uses correct sitting posture while doing classwork at school.

Safety and Accident Prevention

1. Students observe safety rules when using playground facilities. This should become a consistent practice after several lessons in which students analyze the causes of accidents and write a list of rules approved by the teacher and the principal.
2. When using power equipment in shop classes at school, all students use safety goggles.

Oral Health

1. Each student brushes his teeth or rinses his mouth after eating lunch.
2. Fourth-grade students choose foods for snacks that will help clean their teeth, such as celery or carrots.

Drug Use and Abuse

1. When offered a drug by a classmate, the student does not accept it.
2. The student does not take prescription drugs at school unless they are prescribed by his physician.

Vision and Hearing

1. If glasses or corrective lenses have been prescribed for the student, they are worn as needed.
2. Each student wears protective lenses when necessary while participating in athletic events at school.

Higher Cognitive Skills

If the learner is expected to make intelligent health decisions, he must develop higher-level cognitive skills so that he can think critically about health problems and issues. The teacher of health should formulate behavioral objectives that measure the extent to which these cognitive skills have been attained.

Comprehension

The student demonstrates that he understands health information when he applies the skills of translation, interpretation, and extrapolation. Examples of behavioral objectives requiring different skills of comprehension follow:

1. The student can correctly explain in his own words the meaning of each term in a list of terms pertaining to the control of communicable diseases. *(Translation)*
2. Each student in a tenth-grade health class is to incorporate statistical data about venereal diseases into a written paragraph on the frequency of diseases among young people. *(Translation)*
3. After one week of instruction on automobile and pedestrian safety, the student will be able to explain orally the meaning of five standard road signs. *(Translation)*
4. Students incorporate into a diagram the information contained in a paragraph explaining the infectious cycle. *(Translation)*
5. Students write a 100-word paragraph explaining what happened in an experiment they watched showing the effects of cigarette smoke on goldfish. The paragraph should discuss at least two observed effects. *(Interpretation)*

6. After reading a paragraph on the effects of LSD, tenth-grade students are to interpret orally to the class what was said, without referral to the text. *(Interpretation)*
7. Given a hypothetical situation about a person who misused a drug and became addicted to it, the student writes a paragraph indicating how he might feel and react if he were in such a situation, and what the consequences might be. *(Extrapolation)*
8. Students write a 1000-word essay indicating what effects the legalization of marijuana might have on society. The essay should incorporate facts obtained from discussion and reading done on the subject. *(Extrapolation)*
9. Twelfth-grade students are to discuss orally or in writing what life on earth might be like in fifty years if the present rate of pollution continues. Discussions are to be substantiated by data presented in class. *(Extrapolation)*
10. Following two weeks of instruction on the control of communicable diseases, each twelfth-grade student is to write a two-page paper on what life might be like if immunizations were not available. *(Extrapolation)*

Analysis

Analysis refers to the breaking down of information into its component parts. Examples of behavioral objectives in health for this type of cognition follow:

1. Seventh-grade students identify at least two nutrients found in each food on a list compiled by the class. Eighty percent of each student's responses are to agree with data in a manual on nutrition.
2. When shown a picture depicting a home setting with twenty health hazards, the student can identify at least fifteen of these hazards, using criteria established by the class.
3. Students in a eighth-grade health class are to identify at least three unstated assumptions made in a cigarette advertisement shown to them on an opaque projector.
4. Each student who has completed a unit on exercise can correctly name each major muscle group that is involved when the arms and legs are extended and flexed. Answers are to be checked by reference to a text on anatomy.
5. The student is to prepare a written analysis of two case studies involving sexual problems. In each analysis the student should determine the possible causation of the problem and suggest two ways in which the problem might have been avoided.

6. When presented with a hypothetical public health problem, such as an outbreak of measles, and after studying the community in which the outbreak is to have occurred, each student writes a four-page paper in which he identifies at least three factors that could have been responsible for the epidemic.

Synthesis

Synthesis is the rearranging of knowledge into new relationships or products or into existing patterns after it has been analyzed. Examples of health objectives that require this skill follow:

1. Twelfth-grade students are to write three-page papers in which they integrate results of research and investigation from several sources into a plausible plan for solving a given public health problem, such as the misuse of drugs by adolescents.
2. Provided with the regime of an overweight person, including his eating habits, rest periods, sleeping habits, and exercise routines, a tenth-grade student can calculate the number of calories consumed and the number utilized and can develop a balanced program of exercise, rest, and nutrition to enable the person to lose one pound per week for five weeks.
3. Each student who has received instruction on factors that relate to successful marriage develops a list of criteria for selecting a marriage partner and indicates their order of importance to him.

Evaluation

Evaluation is the use of internal or external criteria in making value judgments about information provided. Examples of behavioral objectives emphasizing this area of cognition are:

1. Using a list of criteria provided by the Food and Drug Administration, the student determines whether or not certain health products meet specified standards.
2. By using a list of criteria for determining postural divergencies, the student can decide whether or not a classmate has postural defects.
3. Seventh-grade students determine the extent to which safety rules are practiced in manual-training classes by referring to a checklist on shop safety.
4. Students, using standards established by the Food and Drug Administration, determine the validity of advertised claims for selected health products.

Creative Skills

This type of objective requires the learner to develop original or imaginative solutions to health problems. Not all students in a class should be expected to attain creative skill objectives. The teacher can provide learning opportunities to encourage able students to exercise their creative skills. Examples of creative-skill behavioral objectives in health instruction follow:

1. One-third of the members of a tenth-grade health class develop two alternate plans for solving a public health problem described by the teacher.
2. Following four weeks of instruction on world health problems, four out of thirty students in a twelfth-grade class recommend three ways of solving the overpopulation problem. Responses are to be judged feasible by a panel of students and teachers.
3. Three out of thirty students give two alternate plans for providing adequate nutrients to people throughout the world. They will do this after reading about and discussing major malnutrition problems.
4. Students complete a unit on safety and accident prevention, then create designs for automobiles that would provide complete protection for the passengers in case of accident. Two out of thirty students should submit designs judged unique and feasible by the class.
5. Given data on the extent of the drug abuse problem in a community, four out of thirty students develop two alternate plans for ameliorating the problem.
6. After reading Food and Drug Administration publications about quackery in the United States, two out of thirty students develop plans to eliminate this problem. Responses are to be judged plausible by a doctor or medical student.

Sequencing Behavioral Objectives

As described in the opening chapters, meaningful behavioral objectives should not stand isolated from one another. They should be ordered in some logical sequence, so that one objective relates to another and the student can see meaning and relevance in the objectives he is expected to attain.

Behavioral objectives in health instruction may be developed in a number of sequences that are relevant to the needs and abilities of the student. The teacher might develop a sequence based upon the range of cognitive skills, progressing from lower level to higher level skills. In some instances a sequence might usefully be based upon content areas to be covered. In other cases, the intellectual development of the learner may be used as the basis for sequencing. Finally, a sequence of objectives might relate to a specific concept to be acquired by the student.

Sequencing Based on Cognitive Skills

The following sequence of cognitive skills is an example of one that might be required in the study of nutrition, with specific reference to the four basic food groups. The behavioral objectives cited would take a seventh-grade student through the levels of recall, comprehension, analysis, synthesis, and evaluation.

Recall. After witnessing a flannel-board demonstration, the student can state orally or in writing the four basic food groups.

Comprehension. Given a food group, the student lists foods included in the group and explains orally or in writing why each food group is important to health.

Analysis. When the student is provided with a menu describing the foods eaten by a person for one day, he can classify the foods eaten into four basic food groups.

Synthesis. From a list of foods, the student can compile breakfast, lunch, and dinner menus that contain foods from each of the four food groups.

Evaluation. With the use of a calorie counter and a chart of the four basic food groups, students can determine from the weekly diet and regime of activity of a 150-pound, fifteen-year-old boy whether or not the individual is receiving the recommended allotment of food from each of the four basic food groups and whether or not that individual's caloric intake is in keeping with the amount of energy he expends.

Sequencing Based on Content Areas

In some cases the teacher might consider it important for students to learn about certain content areas before others. To provide this type of learning, a sequence can be based on the order in which content areas are to be covered. For example, the following behavioral objectives in mental health might profitably be attained prior to studying drug abuse:

1. After instruction on factors that influence mental health, the student can state ways in which peers might influence one's behavior.

Because of the attainment of the above behavioral objective, the one following, in the area of drug abuse, might be more meaningful:

2. Following instruction on factors that might contribute to drug abuse, the student explains ways in which social pressures can lead to drug abuse.

These cognitive skill objectives for nutrition could be a prerequisite to those in dental health:

1. Following instruction on minerals and vitamins, the student can list those vitamins and minerals necessary for calcification.
2. Students identify on a list those foods that are high in vitamin D, calcium, and phosphorus.

After these objectives in nutrition have been met, the following dental health objectives might be more easily attained:

1. After instruction on factors influencing the development of dental cavities, the student can explain orally or in writing how a lack of vitamin D, phosphorus, or calcium can influence the structure or development of the tooth.
2. The student can classify a list of foods into those conducive to healthy teeth and gums and those conducive to cavities.

Sequencing Based on Intellectual Development

Behavioral objectives may be arranged in sequence on the basis of the intellectual development of the learner. The three stages of intellectual development described by Piaget[2] is one structure that might be utilized. While an age range is assigned to each of Piaget's stages, it is important to note that the appearance of these stages varies with the individual. These three stages are (1) the *intuitive-thought* stage (ages two to seven), (2) the *concrete-operations* stage (ages seven to eleven), and (3) the *formal-operations* stage (ages eleven-to-twelve to fourteen-to-fifteen).

Intuitive-Thought Stage. In this stage trial-and-error operations occur. The child must have concrete or tangible evidence of that which is to be learned. Lower-level cognitive skills and simple behavioral skills, such as those following, might be applied.

1. The pupil gives the correct name of a fruit upon seeing a model of it.

---

2. See Jean Piaget, *Logic and Psychology* (New York: Basic Books, Inc., 1957).

2. During work or play sessions, the student learns by trial and error to get along with others and demonstrates skill in sharing equipment and toys.

Concrete-Operations Stage. At the next stage, the concrete-operations stage, the child can reason in a logical manner, but he still needs concrete experiences. Higher-level cognitive objectives can be employed here. Building upon the two previous behavioral objectives, these are examples of concrete operations:

1. Following a flannel board presentation in which a number of different cut-outs of food are used in teaching about the four basic food groups, the pupil can arrange ten cut-outs of food into the four basic groups.
2. The pupil acts in an appropriate manner during group activities of play situations, by using trial and error to get along with others.

Formal-Operations Stage. At this stage, the child can formulate hypothetical situations. Given certain information, he can predict what might occur as a result. High-level cognition and creative-skill objectives might apply here. The following examples build upon the intuitive-thought and concrete-operations stages already described:

1. The learner can predict the health problems that might arise as a result of a diet deficient in foods from one of the four basic food groups.
2. When told of a specific social situation and the behavior displayed by one child, the pupil can predict possible reactions of the group to that child.

Sequencing Based on Concept Acquisition

In each health content area, students should be expected to acquire basic concepts. One basic concept may be expressed differently in behavioral objectives at primary, intermediate, junior-high, and senior-high levels.

A sequence of behavioral objectives can be based upon the acquisition of such basic concepts. For instance, a major concept to be acquired by students might be: *food and proper nutrition are important to an individual's everyday functioning.* A number of measurable behavioral objectives, such as those following, could be developed to judge attainment of different phases of this concept. Indications of grade levels appear in parentheses.

1. Following a class discussion on food, the student can state orally or in writing four purposes of food consumption. *(Third grade)*

2. The student can tell which of two foods are used primarily for energy and which primarily for growth. *(Third grade)*

By the time children complete the sixth grade, they can be expected to understand that this concept of proper eating habits can prevent specific health problems. The development of such understanding can be measured by objectives such as:

3. Students state orally or in writing at least one way in which proper nutrition could help prevent each health problem on a list prepared by the teacher *(Sixth grade)*

4. After instruction on the relationship of nutrition and dental health, the student describes at least three ways in which proper nutrition and eating practices help to maintain good dental health. *(Sixth grade)*

When students complete the ninth grade, they can be expected to understand that eating habits can contribute to a number of diseases and disorders. Again, this is an extension of the major concept that food and proper eating practices are important to the individual's functioning. Objectives for the acquisition of this junior-high concept might include the following:

5. Following instruction on the relationships between disease and nutrition, the student lists and describes six major disorders that could be caused by poor eating habits. *(Ninth grade)*

6. The student predicts personal health problems that might develop because of particular eating habits and tells how the community in general might be affected. *(Ninth grade)*

With regard to the same major concept, by the time the students complete the twelfth grade they can be expected to understand that the eating habits of individuals can affect the individual and society. Objectives that help in the acquisition of the concept might include:

7. After two weeks on instruction on nutrition, the student explains how the productivity of a community can be affected by the poor eating habits of its citizens. *(Twelfth grade)*

8. Given the food and eating habits of an individual, the student determines whether or not that person has a balanced diet, and predicts two possible effects upon the health of the individual. *(Twelfth grade)*

Review Questions and Practice Exercises

1. Why should health instruction be an integral part of the school curriculum?

2. Upon what basis should the content of health instruction be determined?

3. What part does the study of anatomy, physiology, and biology play in health instruction?

4. Review the health content areas listed in this chapter. Do these areas include the major health problems of today? If not, what other health problems should be included?

5. Write one or more behavioral objectives for any five of the content areas listed in this chapter. Ask a colleague to review them with you. Each objective should contain the following elements:

    a. Clear description of the behavior sought in the learner

    b. Proficiency level or standard for the behavior.

    c. Conditions under which the student is expected to perform the behaviors sought

    d. Means for determining the extent to which behavioral objectives have been attained.

6. Explain why evaluation is a continuous process in health instruction. In what ways are behavioral objectives a guide to evaluation in health instruction?

7. What is the difference between clinical or subjective evaluation, and statistical or objective evaluation? Give an example of each kind of evaluation for one of the objectives you developed in exercise 5.

8. Name the three kinds of academic objectives that make up the discipline of health instruction. Give at least two examples of each kind of objective for any one of the content areas listed in this chapter. Discuss examples with co-workers. How does each kind of objective differ? In what ways are the objectives similar?

9. Using one or more of the health content areas listed in this chapter, write one behavioral objective for each of the following higher-level cognitive skills: comprehension, analysis, synthesis, evaluation.

10. For any one of the health content areas, write a behavioral objective requiring use of each of the following types of comprehension: translation, interpretation, and extrapolation.

11. Write at least two creative-skill behavioral objectives for any of the content areas listed in this chapter.

12. Working with colleagues, arrange a sequence of behavioral objectives in health based on:

    a. Three or more cognitive skills

    b. Two or more content areas

    c. The intellectual development of the learner

    d. Concept acquisition

Bibliography

Alhambra, Garvey. *Health Education Teaching Guide*. Alhambra, California: San Gabriel School Districts.

Bloom, Benjamin, and Krathwohl, David R., *Taxonomy of Educational Objectives*, Handbook I: *Cognitive Domain*. New York: McKay, 1956.

Cauffman, Joy G. "Effectiveness of Selected Approaches for the Teaching of Health Education," *Synthesis of Research in Selected Areas of Health Instruction*. New York: School Health Education Study, 1963.

Commission on Philosophy, Health Education Division, American Association for Health, Physical Education, and Recreation. "A Point of View for Health Education," *Journal of Health, Physical Education, and Recreation* (1962): 26.

Fodor, John T. and Dalis, Gus T. *Health Instruction: Theory and Application*. Philadelphia: Lea & Febiger, 1966.

Fodor, John T., and Glass, L. H. *A Teacher's Guide — Cigarette Smoking and Health — Grade Six*. Northridge: San Fernando Valley State College, 1969.

Framework for Health Instruction in California Public Schools, compiled by John T. Fodor, Ben C. Gmur, and Wilfred C. Sutton. Sacramento: California State Department of Education, 1970.

Grout, Ruth E. *Health Teaching in Schools*. Philadelphia: W. B. Saunders, 1966.

How Children Develop. Columbus, Ohio: Ohio State University, 1964.

Hoyman, Howard S. "An Ecologic View of Health and Health Education," *Journal of School Health* (1965): 110–123.

Jenkins, Gladys G.; Shacter, Helen; and Bauer, William W. *These Are Your Children*. Chicago: Scott, Foresman, 1966.

Joint Committee on Health Problems in Education of the National Education Association and the American Medical Association. *Why Health Education?* Washington: National Education Association, 1965.

Kilander, H. Frederick. "Evaluating Health Teaching," *Journal of Health, Physical Education, and Recreation* (1961): 40.

Krathwohl, Davis R.; Bloom, Benjamin; and Masea, B. B. *Taxonomy of Educational Objectives*, Handbook II: *Affective Domain*. New York: 1964.

Mager, Robert F. *Preparing Objectives for Programmed Instruction*. San Francisco: Fearon, 1961.

Means, Richard K. *Methodology in Education*. Columbus, Ohio: Charles E. Merrill, 1968.

National Education Association. *Schools for the Sixties*. New York: McGraw-Hill, 1963.

National Society for the Study of Education. 53rd Yearbook. *Integration of Educational Experiences*. Chicago: University of Chicago Press, 1958.

Oberteuffer, Delbert. "Vital Ties Between Health and Education," *National Education Association Journal* (1964): 57–61.

Parker, J. Cecil. "Evaluation of Health Education Activities." *California's Health* (1955): 25–26.

Piaget, Jean. *Logic and Psychology*. New York: Basic Books, 1957.

Piaget, Jean. *The Psychology of Intelligence*. London: Routledge and Kegan Paul, 1950.

Popham, W. James. *The Teacher-Empiricist*. Los Angeles: Tinnon-Brown, 1970.

School Health Education Study. *Health Education—A Conceptual Approach to Curriculum Design*, Washington, D.C.: School Health Education Study, 1967.

Sutton, Wilfred C. "Health Needs, Interests and Problems as a Basis for Curriculum Planning," *Synthesis of Research in Selected Areas of Health Instruction*. Washington: School Health Education Study, 1963.